Foundation for XaaS

Service Architecture in Twenty-First-Century Enterprise

PRAFULL VERMA AND
KALYAN KUMAR

ISBN: 0692688315
ISBN 13: 9780692688311

Updated January 2018

ACKNOWLEDGMENTS

We originally planned to write a book on cloud-service management and even initiated the project. While we were pondering about the content of that book, we found that the most important topic that came up was "as a service" model. We believe it has a vast impact and scope, and it goes beyond IT service or the technology domain. As we started thinking more about the subject, we realized that we needed a separate book dedicated to this topic to give the subject the full justice it deserves. Here is that book, and we hope that readers will find it to be a good read.

Although there are many colleagues and friends who indirectly, through formal discussions and even casual chats, triggered many thought processes in creating this book, I want to specifically acknowledge Rahul Kandhari, who was instrumental in bringing several ideas from my mind onto the paper.

Of course, my wife, Annie, and daughter, Naomi, deserve many thanks for their continued support of my undefined work style.

Prafull Verma

We have been intrigued by the As-a-Service Economy and the Ecosystem enabled business models in the 21st century. This led us to combine multiple topics of interest and write a foundation book to enable a common understanding of XaaS. Although many colleagues and friends who contributed to the conversations both formally and informally over chat I would like specifically name Tajeshwar Singh, Navin Sabharwal, Krishna Kotipalli who were instrumental in the process of bringing clarity into the thinking behind this book. I would like to make a special mention for my dear friend, colleague and band-mate Krishnan Chatterjee for the brainstorming we did for the concept of the Service Exchange and XaaS Foundation. I would specifically like to mention Anant Gupta (CEO of HCL Technologies) whose initiative of the next gen task force led us to the concept and thinking of the 21st Century Enterprise. He has been kind enough to write the Foreword for this Book.

And of course, the continued and unwavering support of my Spouse Zulfia who continues to push me to explore new frontiers and my Little Boy Azlan who will grow up to experience the true As-a-Service Economy in the middle of the 21st century enterprise and whose questions and insights always intrigue me into the future.

Kalyan Kumar

PREFACE
TO THE UPDATED EDITION

For writing and publishing this book, we are following the concept of DevOps used for creating software. In the beginning, the focus of the DevOps is to create a minimum viable product (MVP) and release for the use and then build up the feature and functions (and also fix the bugs) in subsequent releases that can be paced with the market need and the resources of the software builder.

Similarly, in the first release of this book, the idea was to bring in the fundamental concepts of the XaaS to the audience. In last couple of months, we realized the need of additional narratives on several points and added in this updated edition. Although at the time of first release, we knew that more narratives are desirable but we did not have enough time to figure out where and what narratives might be required from reader's perspective, especially when the topic is absolutely a new in the industry. In past few months we got those via the feedback, hence this updated release is composed.

We shall continue to follow the same approach because the modern publishing systems allows to work in this manner and we believe that this is the true benefit of technology in publishing industry.

FOREWORD

In a world where every turn is guided with GPS, we're entering the high noon of a new Service Economy without a clear roadmap.

This is not the service economy as we understood it in the 20th century. This is the API-led ecosphere, with a constellation of applications, where everything is consumed "as a service." This is the world of XaaS, or 'X-as-a-Service' where 'X' stands for everything – or anything!

As a customer, the transformation has been a treat as we enjoy the convenience of receiving quite literally everything as a service – from cars to lodging, from software to hardware, from (cloud) storage to analytics to our most advanced technology requirements.

However, for businesses striving to adapt and succeed in this new space, it is a tougher, much tougher transition. Many are trying to wing it along the way. But with relentless change at a blistering speed, and with little or no precedence for guidance, this is resulting in multiple accidents enroute.

The ones driving through successfully are those transforming themselves into a 21st Century Enterprise (21CE), recognizing the need to change and relook not just at their systems but at their very organization so as to leverage the metamorphosis in the business environment.

The 21CE is built on some basic pillars that ensure a strong foundation for it to succeed in the new environment. At its very core, it applies technology to transform its business model and focus sharply on "outcomes" that cut across value chains, delivering a superior end-to-end experience within complex ecosystems. It is essentially agile and lean for a swift response to changing market conditions. And, irrespective of the sector it operates within, the 21CE is "service-oriented." This book addresses this critical value chain of the 21CE: the service value chain.

Perhaps the first book on the subject written by IT professionals, it offers a comprehensive behind-the-scenes view of the new service economy and leads us step-by-step through the most fundamental aspects of its service architecture, its multi-layered technologies, along with the underlying Autonomics that bind them.

To set the context, Prafull Verma and Kalyan Kumar (or 'KK' as we all know him) first provide a glimpse into the changing backdrop, delving on important changes in the enterprise as well as technology landscape. Having done so, they then take a deep dive into the service transformation we are witnessing in the world of XaaS, unveiling its service architecture, extending across service economics, monitoring and control, support and security.

I truly believe that this book fills an important void in a world perplexed by the pace and scope of change around it. A world that is struggling to adopt a new way of thinking, one that understands and embraces the technology that lies at the heart and soul of the service economy.

Anant Gupta
Former President & CEO, HCL Technologies

TABLE OF CONTENT

1. WELCOME TO TWENTY-FIRST-CENTURY ENTERPRISE 1
   1.1 What Is Changing? 1

2. ENTERPRISE IT STRUGGLING FOR RELEVANCE 8
   2.1 IT/BT/OT 8
   2.2 Legacy IT Service Management 12
   2.3 Intersecting Worlds in the Service Universe 13
   2.4 Digital Business Era 15
   2.5 Era Of Service Beyond IT 17

3. SERVICE TRANSFORMATION 19
   3.1 Welcome to Xaas World 19
   3.2 Where is The Service Architecture? 31
   3.2.1 Various Architectures' Domain and Applicability 33

4. SERVICE ARCHITECTURE FOR XAAS 36
   4.1 Key Components In Service Architecture 39
   4.1.1 Service Function 39
   4.1.2 Service Value Chain 40
   4.1.3 Service Consumption 44

4.1.4 Service Economics..44

4.1.5 Service Usage and Billing 45

4.1.6 Service Monitoring and Control 47

4.1.7 Self-Service...47

4.1.8 Service Support...48

4.1.9 Service Security..49

4.2 XaaS Enablement Through Service Architecture 50

5. NEXT-GEN SERVICE MANAGEMENT
FOR THE XAAS MODEL 52

5.1 New Service Management Approach Needed 52

5.1.1 Thee Relevance of ITIL 53

5.1.2 The Generation of Born Digital 54

5.1.3 User Support Is Out and Service Support Is In. 54

5.1.4 Service Catalog Becomes the Core Of SM 55

5.1.5 Crowdsourcing Is The Key..56

5.2 Approach for Next Gen Service management 56

5.2.1 Start From Service Catalog 57

5.2.2 Catalog Aggregation & Service Orchestration 59

5.2.3 It is Build Vs. Aggregate. 59

5.2.4 It is Fulfilling Vs. Orchestrating 59

5.2.5 Think Of Self-service 60

5.2.6 Think Of BOYD & Mobility 61

5.2.7 Think Of Entitlement-based Delivery 61

5.2.8 Think Of Nirvana State 62

5.3 The Role Of SCDB 63

6. XAAS SYSTEM ARCHITECTURE

6.1 Overview..66

6.2 Important Functional Components 68

6.2.1 Portal...68

6.2.2 Consumer Profile Management 70

6.2.3 SSDSDB (Self-Service Delivery and SupportDatabase) 71

IV

6.2.4 Portfolio and Catalog ----------------------------------- 71
6.2.5 Fulfillment--- 72
6.2.6 Data Stores -- 76
6.2.7 Detection to Correction -------------------------------- 79
6.2.8 Service Chain Entity Qualification ------------------- 79
6.3   Technology For User Experience --------------------- 79

7. SERVICE LIFECYCLE MANAGEMENT
7.1   Building And Deployment ------------------------------ 86
7.1.1 Market Pull--- 87
7.1.2 Demand to Deployment: Creator Push ------------ 89
7.1.3 Request to Fulfillment (R2F)------------------------ 91
7.1.4 Detect to Correct --------------------------------------- 94
7.1.5 Portfolio and Catalog Synchronization ----------- 96
7.1.6 User Registration and Profile Data Maintenance ------ 98
7.1.7 Supplier Registration & Supplier Profile Data Maintenance-- 100

8. XAAS ADOPTION --- 102

9. ITIL, IT4IT, COBIT, AND XAAS---------------------- 112

10. ANNEXURE
10.1 Orchestration And Choreography In IT Operations
       And Service Management ------------------------------ 118
10.2 Importance And Use Cases Of Orchestration ------- 120
10.3 Importance And Use Cases Of Choreography------- 121
10.4 Related Definitions------------------------------------- 122

1 Welcome To Twenty-First-century Enterprise

E nterprises born in the Internet era are fundamentally different from those established in the last millennium. Now, young upstarts (or start-ups), such as Netflix, Amazon, Priceline, Uber, Paypal, and so on, are disrupting age-old business paradigms. But big (and smart) companies are not taking it easy. They are rigorously competing by changing the traditional methods to deliver products and services and by focusing on the customer experience. And the biggest tool they are leveraging is technology. This includes information technology (IT) as the "lubricant" that creates a seamless, frictionless, twenty-first-century business by enabling agility and speed while keeping the business secure and employees productive. The twenty-first-century enterprise enables a truely orchestrated experience enabled via an as-a-service ecosystem underpinned by agile and lean methodologies.

1.1 What Is Changing?

People's appetites for service consumption are increasing dramatically. In addition to the desire to consume more and more, there is a rise in the culture of instant gratification. Consumers want more, and they want it now. Traditional service delivery models cannot fulfill this appetite. Services and delivery models have already changed with the coming of new technologies and new architectures. XaaS is tending to become the de facto delivery model. Here are a few very important trends that are bringing about changes in the business and the enterprises.

XaaS

Pronounced "zaas," XaaS is a collective term said to stand for a number of things, including "X as a service," where X can stand for everything (and anything!). This is a rapidly expanding model not only in cloud service but also in every other industry. It grew from a utility service model and is applied to IT and now non-IT services as well. XaaS is the essence of cloud computing, and the most common examples of XaaS are software as a service (SaaS), infrastructure as a service (IaaS), and platform as a service (PaaS)." These are the new delivery models, and they shall warrant new approaches to service management.

Cloud Domination

Although the traditional IT infrastructure is still the larger part of the infrastructure in every enterprise, and the cloud is a smaller portion, we shall see the trend reverse over time, and the cloud will eventually form the majority of infrastructure. Consequently, the service management approach will also change. Currently, we are using the traditional ITSM system and making some adjustments for cloud-service management. However, in the future, we shall use the cloud-service management system and adjust it for traditional service management.

Explosion in Demand of New Services

The portfolio of services has gone beyond monolithic and standard IT services. Now, there are industry-specific user services that were not thought to be viable in the past. For example, in enterprise IT, we see personal storage on-demand service like Microsoft Onedrive, Google Drive, and Dropbox.

Explosion in Number of Service Providers

The ability to consume services through a mobile device has resulted in a tremendous rise in appetite for service consumption. Organizations cannot possibly scale-up to meet this growing desire and demand for new services, nor can they justify the huge investments required to meet the demand . Therefore, they look for external service providers to provide these services.

Services beyond IT

The need for service integration is not just confined to IT services but applies to any service line. In fact, IT itself will be consumed as a service; for example, a variety of cloud services are actually a derivative of ITaaS.

Enterprise Adapting to the Twenty-first Century

As enterprises prepare for the twenty-first century, (even though we are already there, so it should have already prepared for it, but many have not yet prepared for it), they induce, as well as force, corresponding changes in enterprise IT. Mobility is also driving changes in enterprises. The following are the changing traits of twenty-first-century enterprises:

1. Technology at the core versus technology as the enabler

Historically enterprises have been doing business with established and proven business processes and technology is deployed to automate and enable those business processes. Those business processes are usually designed without the imaginations of emerging technological capabilities and keep technology in the secondary place. Twenty first century organizations, on the other hand are making technology the core of the business, instead of sticking to the old paradigm of using technology as an enabler. So the business processes are designed on the foundation of technology. Gone are the old days when the CEO would leave technology matters to the CIO. How many boards of directors have hired CEOs without knowledge of finance or the product that forms the core of the company's business? Likewise, in the twenty-first century, boards of directors will be compelled to bring in technology-savvy CEOs.

2. Customer versus service consumer

Traditional customers are being replaced by a new generation of consumers who were born in the digital culture and are nurturing the culture of consumerization. Their expectations and demands commensurate with what the "born digital" enterprises can deliver, and there is a huge gap between digital and traditional enterprises. New generations of consumer is driven by the instant gratification, more and more choices, short cycle consumption pattern and desire to have a memorable experience. Today's consumers want the best and want it now. Paradigm of instant gratification has enormous impact on every aspect of the service in the entire service lifecycle. How to design the service that can be quickly deployed and fulfilled almost instantaneously? Digitalization of the business is therefore a business compulsion.

Another aspect of the instant gratification is the desire to consume more and demand variety. Direct impact of instant gratification is that the lifecycle of the products and services are shrinking rapidly in consumer world.

3. Request-driven service versus catalog-driven service and self-service

New-generation service consumers are accustomed to seeing the catalog and making choices. If a service provider has not published a service in the catalog then it is deemed as not available and consumer will not make any effort to enquire about the possible availability against their specific need. It is responsibility and the business compulsion of the service provider to expose the service in the catalog. It is very similar to the buyer behavior in a retail store where they pick up the merchandise that is visible on the shelf and it is retailer's business interest to make is visible to the buyer. For IT service consumer, IT is just as any business service, and there is no reason for any exception because it is a technical system. In fact, every business system is a technical system. In the old days, I would request an the airline agent to provide an aisle seat; now I just select the seat while booking. Previously, I would make a request to a banking agent to initiate a fund transfer; now I use the fund transfer service online. So why should I request my IT service agent to install a printer driver on my laptop?

4. Monolithic software and underlying infrastructure versus cloud and software-defined infrastructure

Traditionally, services are deployed on a single, shared platform. This approach has the advantage of improving performance since all requests (and responses) traverse the required services without leaving the environment. Monolithic infrastructure can be simpler to operate, but it has become a self-serving purpose. In the cloud native world, each service is individually deployed, managed, and scaled. For example, in monolithic infrastructure, capacity management becomes very complex. Application sizing, and the resource capacity optimization of each resource must be taken care. In software defined infra, the capacity management is virtually an inherent feature at the business capacity management layer.

Micro services and containers – Procedural language programming was emphasizing the structural programs and best practice of composing the programs with subroutines and nested subroutines was an essential part of programming discipline. Microservices and container technology has enabled those concepts beyond solo application boundaries and accelerated the build and deploy of new services. MicroServices provide a opportunity to breakup large complex programs into Business capability oriented Small Modules which are Independent in terms of how they execute and deliver a specific Business Function. MicroServices communicate via APIs

5

between themselves and are more choreographed than orchestrated at the technical layer. MicroServices are ideally realized in runtime via Containers which are fully contained Operating Environment. Technologies like Docker/Kubernetes provide the capability to manage the container lifecycle.

5. Managing cost versus managing outcome

Traditionally the focus is cost management and it is directly linked to the output. Output relates to the deliverables produced by task, while the outcome relates to the benefits or the results of producing the output. It is the consequence of output. Outcome is actually the difference produced by output. Outputs, such as revenue and profit, enable us to fund outcomes; but without outcomes, there is no need for outputs. In twenty first century enterprise, IT organizations will be the game changers and not the cost centers anymore. Cost control for business IT is an outdated concept. IT will now be as any other business unit that exists to deliver outcomes to the business.

6. Managing technology versus managing service

Typically, enterprise IT that automates and enables the business service is organized according to the technology layers. Each layer deals with specific class of technology and manages it in isolation. Technology management functions are often outsourced to different service providers. In twenty first century enterprise, technology silos will lose their relevance, and Service Portfolio managers will function as business managers and source the service from internal as well as external service creators. Technology will be either hidden or commoditized.

7. Managing technology versus managing service

Hitherto, the IT service integration is dealing with the integration of multiple technology service providers, however, in twenty first century enterprise, IT service will actually run the business, the matter of IT service integration will automatically become a business service orchestration. For example, Uber is orchestrating different service providers services to compose a new business service.

Digital Business

Most enterprises have started to think about, and many of them have even initiated, new business designs by blurring the digital and physical worlds. This new business design is represented by XaaS and cloud.

2 Enterprise IT Struggling For Relevance

E mployees want uniformity in the way they consume services outside and within the enterprise. Their expectations are set by companies like Uber, Amazon, and banks with automated self-service features. They carry the same expectations at their workplace and find their organization's service delivery model outdated. It is, therefore necessary for all enterprises to provide their employees a similar experience in office as they get outside the business world.

In the beginning of 21st century, CIOs were largely controlling the technology budget of the enterprise. The approach of technology management as against the service management drifted them from agility and business alignment. As a result, shadow IT started growing where business will bypass CIO's domain and directly source and use IT. With the emergence of cloud, especially the SaaS offering, the trend accelerated. Today, in most of the organizations, classic IT is loosing its relevance and CIOs have pressure to respond to maintain the relevance.

2.1 IT/BT/OT

Information Technology (IT) is the collective term that refers to the set of technologies—namely, computers, hardware, software, storage, networks, and communication used for data processing and data communication. ITIL refers to it as ICT, where C denotes communication. MIS (management information systems) and EDP (electronic data processing) systems were the old acronyms used for IT. MIS/EDP started with financial accounting and back-end office data processing; therefore enterprise IT was deemed as a back-office function. However, the business applications are also components of IT. In the modern world, every aspect of business is run with technology; hence, the Business Technology (BT) is indeed the IT of the contemporary world. BT, by definition, means technology that impacts the business's result, and that is what business-aligned IT is. BT is closely aligned with two other terms commonly associated with the solo operation culture of IT and business: IT and business alignment and the consumerization of IT.

Operational technology (OT) is a category of hardware and software used to monitor and manage industrial devices. Historically, OT was used in industrial control systems for chemicals, manufacturing, transportation, and utilities using point-to-point connected and/or standalone systems in isolation. Most of the tools for monitoring or making adjustments to physical devices were mechanical in nature, and those that did have digital controls used closed, proprietary protocols.

Today, however, as physical devices are becoming "smart," and TCP/IP is the universal networking standard that has standardized the network and driven down the costs of networking, there is an increasing trend toward IT/OT convergence. Wireless connectivity has provided administrators in charge of OT with better monitoring systems and the ability to control physical devices remotely. Advances in networking and machine learning have created a radical change, allowing the data that physical devices produce to be analyzed in real time to facilitate autonomy, allow preventive maintenance, and improve up-time.

Internet-capable technology has now made inroads into industrial control systems and has brought challenges like as malware and identity/access control security problems along with it. The difference is that vulnerabilities in an OT system can leave critical infrastructure at risk of industrial espionage and sabotage if not addressed.

Despite massive investments in technologies, most enterprises find it difficult to stay at the top of the industry for long. They fail to understand the next-generation enterprise technology needs as well as performance needs of their customers. The problem is not just restricted to spotting the customers' technology needs but also not having a holistic view of all technology experiences that are delivered to them through various technology spectrums. To be able to deliver next-generation technologies and unified experiences, enterprises must look at the world from customers' perspectives and focus on enterprise technology, which is beyond information technology or business technology. I get restless when enterprises' long-term technology vision focuses on a single technology spectrum; they either have an IT plan, which is often separated from business technology, or may slightly detail out an operational technology. The problem with this type of long-term technology strategy is that even before you realize the actual outcome, you have lost the battle and are outperformed by other enterprises that focus on enterprise technology. We advise CEOs to start investing in enterprise information technology. Enterprise technology is all about supplying a unified experience delivered through various technology spectrums. For twenty-first-century enterprises, it is no longer about IT and/or operational technology; it's about the big convergence of IT, operational, and business technologies. Their vision clearly focuses on building a strong foundation for the enterprise.

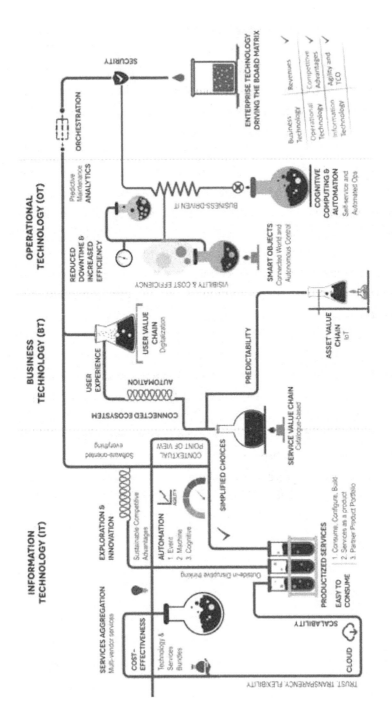

Figure 1: Convergence of IT and BT—technology that supports the convergence

In this dynamic and volatile business world, being the chief of any technology spectrum is more challenging than it ever was. You are expected to predict and automate faster than ever before and with 100 percent accuracy. The good news is that enterprise technology does exactly that; it provides accurate predictability and automation. On top of that, it enables agility and provides the total cost of ownership to help you build the enterprise of the future with next-generation technologies. On top of that, it enables agility and provides the TCO levers to help you build the enterprise of the future with next-generation technologies with a consume first approach. Consequently, enterprise technology contributes massively to the board matrix by delivering agility, revenues, and competitive advantages. It gives you what you need to be at the top of your industry for a long time.

2.2 Legacy IT Service Management

Historically, all the groups and functions in the EDP (electronic data processing) and MIS (management information system) departments were designed for the sole purpose of managing technology. The pervasive acronym of today's world, IT, was nonexistent; consequently, IT service as a concept was also nonexistent. As the concept of IT grew in the 1980s and client server technology proliferated, IT service management found its place in the new IT world—as the new avatar of MIS.

The service management approach secured its strong foundation with the emergence of a formal helpdesk service in the client server era and then with the adoption of ITIL. Contemporary service management frameworks such as ITIL, COBIT, and IT4IT have a strong emphasis on IT service management. Soon after these frameworks started getting traction in the market, ITSM vendors started rolling out products to support these frameworks, which acquired the status of IT service management tools. With the availability and the popularity of service management tools, traditional service management based on ITIL became the de facto industry standard. I have not come across any enterprise that does not have ITIL implemented (maturity is not the matter for discussion here, though).

What is lacking in traditional service management is the catalog-driven service and self-service. Of course, there are many other lacunae (such as the degree of automation, instant delivery, and so on), but these two are the user-driven characteristics, and the user is the center of the service universe around which everything revolves.

In the client server era, each application had a client component, which has to be installed to use the application. Internet browsers killed the concept of application-specific clients in a client server architecture. Browsers became the universal client for all applications. Now, individual apps are coming back as the focused solution for provider-specific service consumption components.

2.3 Intersecting Worlds in the Service Universe

The consumer world dominates as the focus shifts from left to right in the intersection service world shown in diagram 1 below.

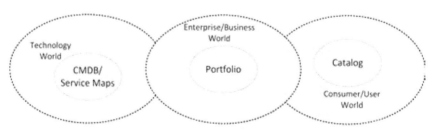

Intersecting worlds in the service universe

Figure 2: Shifting focus on service worlds

Even though the service management frameworks have a strong emphasis on service management, technology management remained the dominant part in all IT organizations. The concept of CMDB—the database of configuration items and their inter relationships—became the universe of internal IT. The technology world (i.e. The IT professionals who develop, deploy and maintain technology infrastructure) focuses on physical components and revolves around the CMDB. Each technology vendor, along with its products, offered tools to manage that technology. VMware vRealize and SAP SOLMAN are just a couple of examples. Technologists are usually excited with newer products that are technically refined and technically superior to those of the previous generation. They wanted to incorporate the new technology with an assumption that it will deliver better service, but that is not necessary. Technology is not the solution for every problem; it is just one of the components.

With service management, the concepts of service portfolio and service catalog also got visibility. Although application portfolio was maintained by many organizations, it was still technology-oriented, and ITIL added the service portfolio layer on top of the application. Service portfolio became the center of the universe in ITIL v3 for the business world and was focused on the business alignment and cost models. Since the business pays for the production, delivery, and support of the services, its focus is on Return on Investments (ROI) and Return on Capital Employed (ROCE). In enterprise IT, business managers are the real customers, not the users.

Until this era, the end-user technology in the corporate environment had an edge in the sense that users have better technology at work compared to what they would have at home. The equation started changing after 2005, and with the arrival of iPhone and mobility applications, personal technology's superiority increased dramatically. Users' behavior changed, and so did their expectations. The only purpose of the service consumer is to use/consume the published service; therefore, the user world is focused on consumption models and revolves around the service catalog. The consumer is looking for ease of accessing and using the service and the experience in using the service. Now the corporate world is under pressure from their employees to provide them with the same level of experience while consuming internal services. The Service Catalog is derived from Service Portfolio. The portfolio is business-to-business (B2B) matter and catalog is business to consumer matter (B2C).

2.4 Digital Business Era

According to Gartner, "Digital business is the creation of new business designs by blurring the digital and physical worlds. Digital business promises to usher in an unprecedented convergence of people, business, and things that disrupts existing business models—even those born of the Internet and e-business eras."(http: // www.gartner.com / it-glossary / digital-business/)

Customers expect speed and personalization. And they are hungry for choices. Digital technology is leveling the playing field for businesses of all sizes and creating opportunities to develop products and services that were once inconceivable. The large size of an enterprise, which was once a competitive advantage, is becoming a liability because of inertia as businesses that once dominated the market are now struggling to keep up with start-ups. The rise of digital is going to disrupt businesses completely and dramatically change the competitive landscape. Today, all enterprises know that to thrive, they must transform into a digital business.

Connect Everything

Connecting everything is the key to digital business.

Within the enterprises that are developing products and services, connecting people, processes, things, and data across the company is the cornerstone of a digital business. It is the ubiquitous collaborative nature of the organizations which enables them to discover unprecedented insights and deliver the experiences that delight; it's ubiquitous collaboration. When everything from R&D, operations, marketing, and sales through to the end customer are connected, businesses are not only more nimble and better informed, but they are able to transform themselves and their relationships with customers.

Today, enterprises are predominantly using legacy heterogeneous IT infrastructure, and cloud is a relatively small part in the overall infrastructure landscape. The traditional ITIL based ITSM are adequate to manage the operations and can handle the cloud-service management and utility service models with viable adjustments.

Tomorrow, most enterprises will use cloud-based infrastructure and utility service models for managing the operations. In such a scenario, new ITSM system for XaaS management will be imperative, and some adjustment will be required to manage the legacy infrastructure.

XaaS Strategy—an Imperative for Digital Transformation

One of the critical aspects of digital business is the virtual necessity of productizing the services. If you are selling a product, it is very easy to answer a customer's question: "What are you giving me?" But it is not that easy when you are selling services.

XaaS enables the productization of service and therefore improves manageability of the business aspects of the service. In our first publication, "Process Excellence for IT Operations," we discussed in detail product versus service and explained the complexity of service because of various factors, including intangibility and perishability. In this section, we would like to talk about some important points about how productization for XaaS supports digital strategy.

Measured by data versus measured by experience

Product quality is measured by data, while service quality is measured by the experience. Historically, user experience was an ignored aspect, at least from the measurement perspective. Digital business has brought the user experience to the center stage. Although user experience is not easy to measure, but by productizing a service, the measurement methodologies will be simplified, thereby improving the manageability. (I repeat the principle that we emphasize in the first publication: If you can measure, you can manage.)

Measuring output versus measuring outcome

While making or manufacturing a product, the output is measured in hard numbers by fundamental units of measurement, but service outcome is measured using derivative measurement units and equations. Similarly, digital business is also emphasizing outcome and shall require simplified measurements. Productization of service enabled by XaaS will make it simple to measure the outcome as well.

Repeatable versus customizable

Another aspect of product management and product business is repeatability. Digital business is also asking for a change in design thinking that will replace the need for customization of a service with the ability to personalize a service. Elements of productization will help both the service creator and consumer; services will be designed for standardized delivery (and therefore repeatability) but will be consumed in a personalized manner.

Patent for a product versus patent for a service

Patents for products are easy to obtain, compared to a patent for a service. Digital business is expected to bridge the gap. Many products are digital and patented as products. Gradually, the productization of service in the digital world will level the playing field for product and service providers.

2.5 Era of IT Service beyond IT

The evolution of technology in the twenty-first century is making technology a core in every enterprise or consumer offering. With the digitalization of the traditional business processes/models, it has become even more evident that IT capability has now become key to the survival of any business. Just like electricity, core technology capability is now taken for granted, and it is expected to be perpetually available on. So every twenty-first-century business service is an IT service; hence, the service management aspect of the entire ecosystem will be at the core of the success of all these new businesses. We also see that with the advent of IOT/connected devices, the dependency on core IT will extend to every connected node in the ecosystem.

3 Service Transformation

A nything as a service, or XaaS (also known as everything as a service), refers to the wide variety of services offered as utility models over the Internet, primarily on the cloud-computing platforms. XaaS reflects the vast potential for various on-demand services like software as a service (SaaS), Storage as a Service, Desktop as a Service (DaaS), Disaster recovery as a Service (DRaaS), Network as a Service (NaaS), Infrastructure as a Service (IaaS), Platform as a Service (PaaS), and even emerging services such as Marketing as a Service and Healthcare as a Service. The end purpose of XaaS is to be provide business ready catalog services which can be consumed directly or configured across multiple services to create a composite Service. The level of Abstraction of XaaS can start from pure cloud technical aervices like IaaS/PaaS to more consumable application functionality in SaaS and truly leading to consuming either a process utility or a function utility service or data Utility... the goal is to move Everything-as-a-Service and shift the focus towards experience and Outcome via User centric or Asset Centric Value chains Or a combination of both.

3.1 Welcome to XaaS World

XaaS is catching up fast because it provides quality service, fast ramp-up, and predefined yet flexible pricing. These services have an effective value proposition and can handle variable demand. For consumers, they are easy to start and stop and do not tie them to long-term contracts.

Typical traits of XaaS are:

1. Catalog driven

A simple rule for XaaS is what cannot be catalogued, cannot be offered. Unlike many implied services in many enterprises, XaaS mandates explicit definitions of offering and transparent metering and billing. A service published in the catalog may be perpetual or one-time transaction-based, but it must be cataloged. Catalog is the top down approach for a new service design. It is the beginning point in the design cycle. With catalog as the beginning point, the business alignment of IT comes by default in service design and service fulfillment. Catalog has become the universe around which everything revolves. If a service is not published in the catalog then it is as good as non-existent service, as there is no other mechanism to request it.

2. Low barriers to entry

The low barrier is not just in terms of the financial parameters but also from the size of the service and the size of the provider. You can be a part of a larger ecosystem and enter into the game with a small part. The model, by design, levels the playing field. Microservice to mega service can coexist in the same catalog. Or even for the same service, the billing revenue may be a few dollars to a few thousands of dollars. There is no constraint on the size of the provider. It does not require large capital or a long time to build and publish a service.
The other aspect is low barrier is from the consumer's side. A consumer can start consuming without any constraint on location, device and time. There is no complex prerequisite to consume service.

3. Little or no capital expenditure—cloud based

XaaS is an inherently cloud-based offering; hence, it requires no capital expenditure. Elimination of capital expenditure removes several financial barriers for the service providers and thus allows expanding the portfolio quickly. Besides this the trend is to use DevOps with little expenditure to come out with a minimum viable product (MVP) and then start build over it as the business demand grows.

4. Massive scalability

Massive scalability is one of the critical requirements in the XaaS world as increasing number of consumers will demand even more services. This is yet another reason that cloud-based service is the de facto deployment architecture.

5. Multitenancy

Multi-tenancy is the core tenet of cloud computing. It helps service provider to share the underlying platform for producing and delivering services to multiple customers. Each customer is logically separated but governed by the same service standards and SLAs. It helps the service provider to maintain a uniform standard at a lower cost, which can be extended to customers.

6. Device independence

The service consumption endpoints have no bearing on the consumer's ability to consume service. Services, by design, are consumer-device agnostic.

7. Location independence

The ubiquity of the Internet makes service delivery as well as service consumption occur anywhere.
In the XaaS world, all services need not be perishable. A commercial model can be created for offering durable service also—for example, pay-by-use hardware-offering models.

8. Infrastructure fault tolerance

Underlying infrastructure on which a service is running is can fail, even in the cloud, and service design criteria are cognizant of this reality. Container and micro service approaches in application building and deployment are addressing these criteria. This reminds me of the history of TCP/IP and packet switching, the backbone of the Internet. Packet-switching technology is the foundation of the fault tolerance of the Internet. Until 1980, all long-distance communication was based on circuit-switching technology. The DARPANET project was founded with the idea of developing the fault-tolerant communication system that would continue to work even if the circuits are broken by enemy attack. The success created the foundation of today's Internet and cloud computing.

Roles in XaaS Model

When anything and everything is offered as a service, then utility models will be pervasive, and three different perspectives will continue to exist:

- Consumers will demand more and more niche services focused on very specific outcomes.
- The market will see a large number of niche service creators meet the growing appetite of consumers.
- We shall see new entities in the service delivery chain to take the services to consumers.

Considering these points, we arrive at three fundamental roles: service consumer, who will consume services; service creators, who will create services; and service orchestrators, who will be the channel between the creator and the consumers. With this consideration, we present a simplified view of the XaaS system in the figure below.creator and the consumers. With this consideration, we present a simplified view of the XaaS system in the figure below.

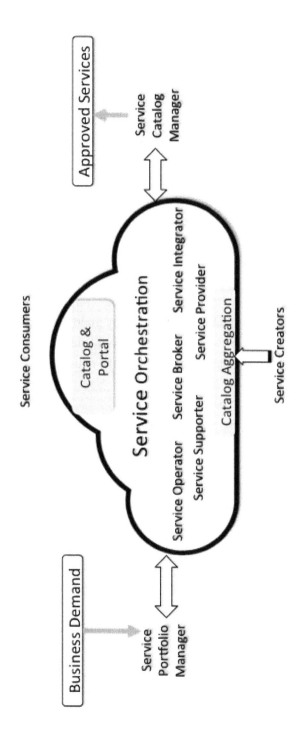

Figure 3: Overview of XaaS system

A Service Catalog is the center of the business world around which everything will revolve. The catalog will always be launched on a portal that will have all the functionality that a service consumer needs to conduct his or her business. If there is a catalog, there must be a portfolio from where the catalog will be derived. That means we expect two more operational roles—namely, portfolio manager and the catalog manager for the operation of the XaaS system.

The existence of a large number of service creators implies the need of catalog aggregation. Regardless of the method of aggregation, the outcome to consolidate individual creators' services is a necessity, and this would be under the governance of a portfolio and catalog manager.

The middle layer between the creator and consumer is the service orchestration function that will be realized by multiple discrete roles. The number of roles required to orchestrate would depend on the kind of service and the commercial model between the entities. We shall take this up in more detail in later sections.

Futuristic CIO Use Case for IT Services

We cite the example of Expedia, which does not run any airline but offers services of all the airlines. If I have to travel from Raleigh to Chicago, Expedia will present me with options from more than one provider. Similarly, in a hypothetical case, instead of producing an in-house personal storage service, a CIO can plug the Google Drive service or Dropbox service in the catalog and outsource the service production, delivery, and support to different entities and just be the orchestrator and/or integrator. This scenario looks theoretical in IT, but it is very well established in other businesses, including Amazon. Then why not in enterprise IT?

XaaS Is the New Philosophy

The XaaS world brings a new philosophy in service management. Let's take a business scenario of an online order system workflow, as shown in the diagram below.

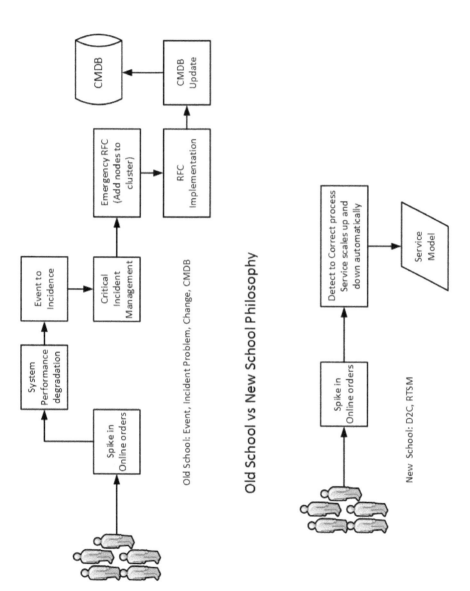

Figure 4: New service management philosophy

When the workload on the order management system spikes, a performance degradation of the transaction system would usually create an incident in the ITSM system via the event-monitoring tool. After some time, someone (usually the service desk or command center) would upgrade the severity of the incident, and the Critical Incident Management (CIM) process will get initiated. Teams will collaborate and determine the need for adding two transaction servers in the cluster (usually one node in the cluster would have been sufficient, but teams want to play it safe). There would be an emergency RFC, and its implementation will resolve the incident and trigger the CMDB update.

Everyone is happy after at least ten people have spent over four hours to get a great sense of achievement and satisfaction. It is a demonstration of a good ITIL processes—event management, incident management, problem management, change management, and CMDB at work.

What has not been accounted for here is that:

1. By adding nodes to the cluster, the license compliance of the application is violated.
2. After the peak load is vanished, the systems will continue to run with overprovisioned infrastructure and will cost more.

Contrary to this, in the XaaS model, there is no team to deal with cluster and nodes because the service is running in the cloud, and the underlying infrastructure is scalable. The service performance is monitored, and as soon as an event is detected, the D2C process automatically scales up to deliver the agreed outcome. As soon as the peak load vanishes, the infrastructure scales down automatically, and billing of services reduces.

Frankly speaking, the virtual environment using vRealize's auto scale feature can very well achieve the foundation of a new school. While virtualization may be used to provide cloud computing, and thus the XaaS service model, cloud computing and XaaS are quite different from virtualization. Cloud computing may look like virtualization because it appears that your application is running on a virtual server detached from any reliance or connection to a single physical host. And they are similar in that fashion. However, cloud computing can be better described as a service, whereas virtualization is part of a physical infrastructure.

XaaS impact on traditional support operations

Figure 5 illustrates how XaaS is impacting the traditional service desk and command center operated support management. The support operations are triggered by an event (that could be an alert or incident) originated fro the malfunction of a configuration item. Command center is usually the single point of contact for dealing with the CI generated incidents. Command center would route the incident to level 1, level 2 or level 3 resolvers and perform the critical incident management if required. This we depicted in figure 4 also. The entire command center would be eliminated because of self-healing design and intelligent automation.

When we analyze the user-originated triggers for support operation that starts with service desk as a single point of contact, we can classify into five buckets all of these buckets can be eliminated by three factors- BYOD, Self Service and Service Catalog.

1. Device support – Enterprises provide standard end user devices usually desktop, laptop or in some cases mobile devices. Since the devices are owned by the enterprise, the support and maintenance responsibility lies on the enterprise. Hardware breakdowns on the devices are rare, but the support related to the device configurations or device setting is enormous. If users were bringing their own devices, then device support would be non-existent. This is very much possible if the service is designed as device independent service.

2. Application Support – Users seek lot of application support in traditional environment. There are two problems here. One the

traditional application is not designed from self-serviceability point of view and has little self-service components. Second, even if the self-service components are feasible, the self-service system is not implemented. In modern design, both the problems are addressed and the need of application support is eliminated.

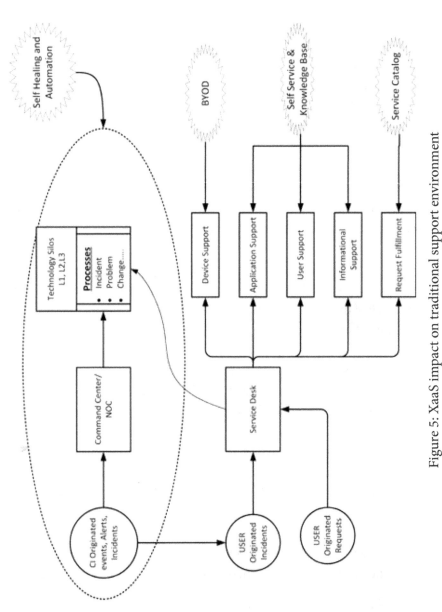

Figure 5: XaaS impact on traditional support environment

3. User Support- Each user can present a unique problem depending upon the way he or she uses the service. Enterprise service desk are designed around user support that usually crosses across all service boundaries. In XaaS world, it would be a matter of service support rather than the user support. The service supply chain would define specific support entity for specific service. Also each service will have personalization features. For example, if you buy a Dell Laptop and call Dell product support that Wi-Fi is not working, the technician would perform the laptop diagnostic and solve device specific issue if any. Technician wills advice you to contact Wi-Fi service provider if device is good and problem persists. In our personal life, we are accustomed to obtain support from different service providers and still work productively. How many times you have called Google for e-mail support or Dropbox for personal storage support? We expect similar approach in enterprise also, as the pampering of users will go away and true service support will take over. This will eliminate user support bucket also.

4. Informational Support- This kind of support includes "how to" question and educational/training support on using the services. This is lack of self service and knowledge base associated with the service. Have you ever called airline and asked how to book ticket or select the seat? Have you ever asked how to download and play a game on your iPhone? We expect similar approach in enterprise that will kill informational support bucket also.

5. Request fulfillment – Users contact service desk with variety of demands such as password reset, account provisioning, share access and so on. All these are the actually the service catalog items. A good service catalog will offer users to browse catalog, order and get fulfilled also.

Illustration of Home IT experience and Enterprise IT experience

Every home is not running its own IT infrastructure and producing internal services as well as consuming external services including business services. Let us illustrate a typical home IT environment and I want to use my own example. I have a home network of laptops of all family members. Family uses Windows and Macbook and each laptop has different OS image. There are tablets and iPhones on the network as well. All of these utilize common Internet services, common WiFi services and print services. This infrastructure uses TWC Internet services. Family members use personal banking services from Bank of America and Wells Fargo. The mail service is provided by Google and Yahoo. Personal storage anytime anywhere from any device is provided by Dropbox and Google. Important point to note

1. I can conduct most of my business with bank via self-service. There is rarely any need to have personal interaction. Bank does not force me to use any specific device for consuming personal banking service online.
2. I use self-service for mail and storage. I never have to call Google Service Desk or Dropbox service desk
3. I use device vendor support for failure of the device but the support is limited to device. They do not support the issue outside the laptop. Like wise TWC does not support WiFi router, the support stops at the termination point of Internet service.
4. I do have service support from individual service providers but I do not have user support. There is no user service desk to pamper me yet I believe I have good service support.
5. I use Internet as my knowledge repository and that provides crowd sourcing of knowledge for problem resolutions.

Why my experience with home IT is better than my enterprise IT? As an individual, I will cite three key reasons – BYOD (Liberation from restriction of enterprise), Self Service and well-designed service (banking service for example). Pampering by user support service desk does not improve my user experience. So it is better for CIO to focus on these three aspects rather than pampering the users and think that they will be happy.

3.2 Where Is The Service Architecture?

Current ITSM is adequate for traditional Service Management that is using CMDB and service maps. This is perfectly fine as long as you have the end-to-end ownership and visibility of all the components in the service maps. A graphical map of interconnected CI—the service map—is good enough to gain a good understanding of service. There are many technological components in that map across different technologies. Most organizations are still technology-focused and maintain different technology architectures (system architecture, network architecture, application architecture, and the like), but they have no focus on service management architecture. Industry-standard Service Management frameworks such as ITIL and COBIT are perceived as service management architecture.

In the XaaS world, a service map will lose much of its significance because the focus will be shifted from mapping the service end-to-end to cataloging the service and service consumption components. XaaS will drive in the need for service architecture in addition to the enterprise service management architecture. While a Service Management architecture describes the Service Management system (process, function, and tools) to manage the lifecycle of the service, service architecture describes the service composition and makes it consumable and transportable in the service chain by design. The service architecture that we are discussing here does not talk about the technical construct of the service. We have considered that as a part of technology management and included in the application architecture.

Service and Service Management Architecture

Architecture as a discipline originated from civil engineering centuries ago and is defined as the art or practice of designing and constructing buildings. Later, this term was expanded to mean design and construction of things beyond civil engineering.

In the information technology area, initially it was applied to computers and then further expanded to network, applications, and software to specify the overall structure, logical components, and logical interrelationships of a computer, its operating system, a network, and application. Architecture can be a reference model such as the open systems interconnection (OSI) reference model that includes every layer, from hardware to the user-interface part of the software, or it can be specific product architecture such as that for manufacturer-specific CPU (Intel Xeon, for example) or a manufacturer-specific operating system (IBM OS/400, for example).

Very often, the term "architecture" is mixed with design, but the design has less scope than architecture. Architecture is a design, but every design is not architecture. A single component or a new function has a design that has to fit within the overall architecture (for example, individual component designs in client server architecture). A similar term, "framework," can be thought of as the structural part of an architecture. In the Service Management area, ITIL, IT4IT, and COBIT are examples of the frameworks upon which each organization is architecting its service management systems.

Architecture is influenced by the organization (customers and users), technical environment, and even the architect's experience.

Our fundamental definition of a service is "service is the set of benefits realized by the execution of a set of activities by a function (persons) or by machines (configuration items), or by both." It is true across all industries and it will never change. Therefore, the set of activities will form the core of our service architecture; however, surrounding the set of service-producing CIs forming the service map/physical model of service, the logical and conceptual model of a service describing service properties and realized by the data model will actually be the holistic service architecture.

Why Is Service Architecture Needed Now?

An XaaS environment will require radically different consideration to architect and design a service. The traditional service map approach will not be sufficient to deal with the XaaS requirements and service portability for XaaS. Additional service properties like, the completeness of the service chain with end-to-end links and metering and billing become mandatory

Service architecture also becomes important when you think beyond technology and think of business services. Also think of the digital world, where IT is the mainstream business, not the enabler. XaaS would be the de facto business model, and service architecture would be critical.

Service Management Architecture versus Service Architecture

Service Management Architecture	Service Architecture
· Helps to manage the service lifecycle from strategy to operation · Depicts the interconnection of entire service management system that includes processes, underlying technologies (systems and tools), and functions	· Part of toolkit in service strategy phase of service management lifecycle · Helps to design the service for consumption purposes · Depicts the different elements/components of a service and relationship

Table 1: Service architecture versus service management architecture

3.2.1 Various Architectures' Domain and Applicability

We have seen that the mention of architecture in IT has become widespread and to some extent has been overtly abused; hence, the position/relevance of architecture is quite confusing in the technology ecosystem. I would like to mention a book on microservices by Sam

Newman as well as his website (http://samnewman.io), where he mentions the approach of a town planner versus an architect. I think the concept of zoning and managing the intersections between different technology-powered business services seems to be the right direction. Also, I think the concept of having one business and service architecture and everything else as a design model, which keeps evolving as the overall architecture keeps evolving, is the direction. We cannot have too many architectures' boundaries leading to too many internal conflicts. We have provided a good guidance on Service Management architecture in our book "Process Excellence for IT Operations".

We would like to really try to simplify the architecture layers in the new XaaS context. The following are what we envision:

1. Business strategy and direction, which includes direct business metrics, that would all drive the formation of business/digital/product architecture—This is the only area where there would be guidelines/boundaries defined at the business domain level.
2. Service architecture, which defines the foundation of XaaS—If the new way of delivering capability and outcomes is underpinned by a service model, then everything needs to be modeled as a service. All aspects related to the orchestration of all these moving, fluid components/services will be determined here.
3. Solution design that would include all aspects of product, function, domain-specific definitions, requirements, and boundaries—These architectures and principles would be directly linked to business strategy/goals, and there isn't any alignment aspect. It is a direct 100 percent derivative, so the concept of business–IT alignment doesn't even exist.
4. Technology/platform/nonfunctional design, which includes all aspects of application/microservices/platform/infrastructure/operations.
5. Security design would still be called out specifically, which would define the overall security/risk and compliance-related architecture that derives from all aspects of product/business to operations and service lifecycle.

6. Target operating model that would define how all these components would run as a lifecycle which is enabled with service management architecture.

It is also important to clarify the boundary and connection between architect and design. As stated earlier, architecture is a design, but every design is not architecture. A single component or a new function has a design that has to fit within the overall architecture. Architecture will dictate the individual component function and interface with other components in the architecture, but it cannot and will not dictate how the design of individual components realizes that function.

4 Service Architecture for XaaS

Not every service is suitable for the XaaS model. Typical characteristics of a service in the XaaS model are:

Service is outcome focused
The focus of the XaaS service is the outcome, rathervthaen the activities and method to bring the outcome. "What do I get?" rather than "what is the provider doing?" is the mind-set of the consumer. That means architecture should depict a clear consumption component and offering.

Service is standardized
The service provider controls service specifications, and the consumer has no say in customization. However, the consumer has a personalization option in most of the services. Standardization is essential for manageability and the agility for service upgrades. That means the architecture should depict a clear function and purpose of the service.

Service delivery is largely automated
Since service is standardized and catalogued, the delivery of service is absolutely deterministic and can be automated. Technology is advanced enough to enable that. That means the complete orchestration chain from creator to consumer is connected and no link is missing.

Self-serviceable

We are seeing an increasing trend in adoption of self-service and automation in businesses that, earlier, had been human delivered. That means service architecture should have a placeholder for every self-serviceable component.

Service is ready to use

This means that the services are already created, offered, with a clear use case and targeted customer segments. It may not be an end consumer but an intermediary who can value add to another intermediary or an end consumer. The architecture perspective of this paradigm is that all entities in the service chain—from consumer to creator—are connected.

Service is charged usage-based

This implies that for every service, the architecture must address the instrumentation, usage monitoring, and billing components.

All of the above points require service design thinking from a service architecture perspective. Figure 6 below depict the service architecture for the XaaS model.

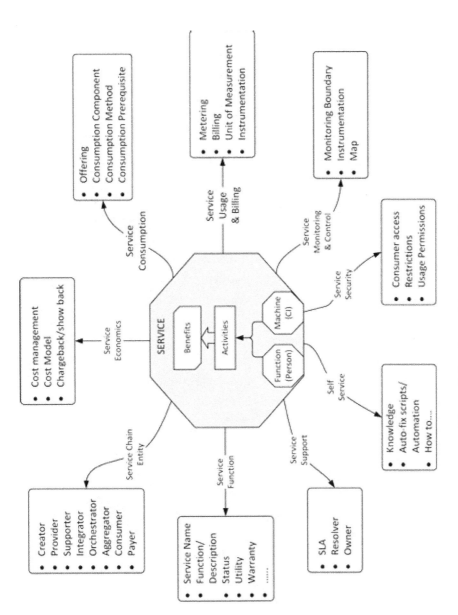

Figure 5: Service architecture for XaaS

The nucleus for producing the service is the set of activities and machine (CI in ITIL terms). The nucleus represents the core service definition—set of benefits produced by activities performed by a machine or person, or both. Attached to this nucleus are the nine logical components used to build a complete view of a service. These components are described in the next section. A complete view of the nucleus is not available even in CMDB or the service map because they focus on the machine part of the service. The person or the role part lies with the processes (technical process or the service management process).

4.1 Key components in Service Architecture

Not all, but a few, of these components are defined as the service attributes in a typical service portfolio in ITIL framework. Besides, ITIL does not envisage the utility model of service; therefore, even if the component is defined as an attribute in the portfolio, the XaaS approach is missing. In our architecture, a component represents a bundle of properties, and some of these properties can be mapped with the attribute in the ITIL portfolio. Also, all the properties and attributes are exhaustive, and, depending upon the lifecycle management and control requirements, more attributes or the properties can be added in the respective areas. We have defined nine areas, and we believe these nine areas make the complete service architecture.

4.1.1 Service Function

Function represents the practical use or the purpose for which a service is designed. In nontechnical terms, it is the description of what a service does for the customer. We use multiple properties or attributes to describe a function, and a few important functional properties are:

1. Name—the identification for a service such as a host name for a CI in the nucleus. This information is used for quick reference and identification.

2. Description—the purpose and the benefits of the service explained from the consumer point of view, as this will be visible to the service consumer.
3. Summary—the summary of the earlier property to serve consumers with a quick view, and, if required, they can drill in details for description.
4. Service Type or Service Class—service category and subcategory are used for grouping the services at different levels distinguished at the group level.
5. Service Utility—service utility defines the fitness for the purpose. It is important to note that in the XaaS world, services are designed for very specific purposes rather than for a general purpose.
6. Service Warranty—a service warranty assures that the service is fit for use. It is tied to the availability of the service.
7. Service Rating—consumers rate the services based on a variety of factors, and the cumulative rating guides the service consumer to make a buying decision. It also helps the service creator to make it better.

Many other properties can be included in functional attributes, such as status, business value, termination date, commencement date, and applicable compliance, as long as these attributes serve specific purposes in the design and publication.

4.1.2 Service Value Chain

Service value chain is defined as the series of roles that carry the service from the service creation point to the service consumption point.

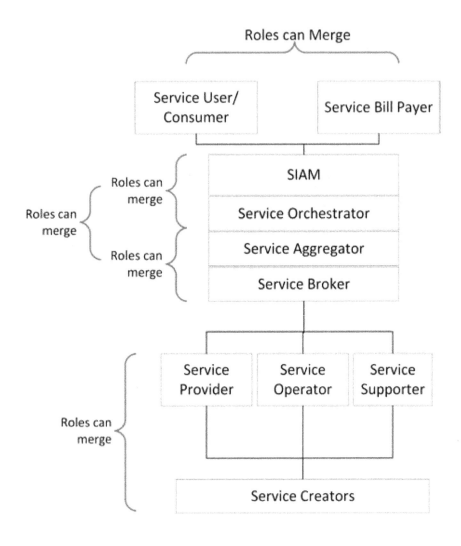

Figure 6: Service chain entities

1. **Service Creator**—The service creator is first, and the creation role is at the origin. This entity is the copyright or IP owner of the service. A service creator may create a service that may not be consumable as is and may require some integration or packaging with other services. A

creator may choose not to deliver service directly to the consumer and may require one or more roles to take it further. A creator may create a service with a trigger of a business demand or may, on his or her own, proactively create and publish in the market and create demand later. For example, a business entity may create an IaaS service without any prior order from any customer and make it available through a cloud broker. We also see many business examples like this one (Gojet Airlines creates the service between Raleigh and JFK, but it is offered by Delta Airline).

2. Service Provider—A service provider is the fulfiller of the service to the service consumer. Every service will have one or more consumption components that can be delivered or fulfilled by one or more provider. We can interchangeably use the terms "service deliverer," "service fulfiller," or "supplier" for the provider role. A service provider is accountable to the service consumer and is exposed directly to the service consumer. Sometimes a provider can be a one-time service-provisioning role, and afterward, the responsibility is handed over to the service operator.

3. Service Integrator—A service integrator brings together two or more individual services and presents them as a single service to the service consumer. The integrator role brings value addition to service offering. The individual services that an integrator is integrating may also be part of the catalog. For example, a SaaS provider may be sourcing IaaS. In end-to-end service delivery and support integration, we also refer to the integrator as the SIAM (Service Integration and Management) role to emphasize its responsibility for delivering or administering end-to-end service across all services that are getting integrated through this entity.

4. Service Operator—A service operator runs, maintains, or operates the service on a day-to-day basis. Typically, in cloud service this is the entity who is maintaining the infrastructure and guaranteeing the availability and performance. A provider can also be an operator. We see this model

quite often in the airline business,. A service provider airline may have multiple independent operators for different sectors; they own and operate the service for a particular flight.

5. Service Support—This role is focused on consumer support and may be outsourced to yet another entity. A service support role can undertake the support for multiple operators/providers or even creators. Think of a single point of contact service desk for this role. In the business world, it is commonly an outsourced call center function.

6. Service Broker—A service broker is usually a reseller who passes on the service to the consumer without changing its form. The service broker role has much more commercial importance and commercial purpose and does commercial value addition.

7. Service Aggregator—The aggregator role is bundling or packaging services into one unit for offering. An aggregator does not change the individuality of the services. In some cases, consolidation is required for delivery or commercial benefits.

8. Service Consumer—The consumer is the end target of the service chain that consumes the services.

9. Service Orchestrator—The orchestrator is a kind of integrator who used completely automated methods to integrate the services in runtime.

10. Service Bill Payer—A bill-paying entity actually pays the bill for the service consumed by the consumer.

Thin Lines between the Value Chain Roles

The integrator, aggregator, and orchestrator roles have very thin lines between them, and it is rare to find a business entity that is an absolute player in one of these roles only. In multiservice-providing scenarios, there are rare cases also where an aggregator is different than the integrator and orchestrator. Very often, these are mixed, and roles terminologies are used interchangeably. Similarly, there is a thin line between the operator, provider, and supporter, and these roles are often combined or used interchangeably.

4.1.3 Service Consumption
Typical service consumption properties are defined by as follows:

1. Service scope or the coverage and what is included and what is not included. Because of the intangibility of the services, this becomes important. For example, in PaaS service, JDK (Java Development Kit) is included, but JRE (Java Run Time) is not included. In business service illustration, we often see airline exclusion of onboard Wi-Fi service.

2. Prerequisite defines the dependency of the service on other factors. Dependency checking is a function that is performed to ensure that all prerequisites for a given runtime image are present. For example, dependency-checking software verifies that all components (even those with low visibility) are present on the client's side. A service will usually have a dependency-checking tool to determine whether all components have been included to deliver the desired outcome. Included dependencies might be device drivers, user interfaces, databases, operating system features, frameworks, certificates, files, or other items.

3. Consumption method will define the procedural part of utilizing the service at the consumption end point that could be a device or a person (for example, in PaaS service, how to configure the user environment to make it suitable for running the service).

4. Items delivered refer to what the consumer will be left with when the service is delivered.

4.1.4 Service Economics

There is a cost involved to build and run service and somebody has to pay for it. Service economics define the cost-management aspects of a service. Service economics help the stakeholders (different roles in the service chain entity) to determine the financial cost, and benefits, of the service. A typical set of attributes related to service economics are:

1. Cost models that define how the service cost is calculated
2. Chargeback or the show back depending upon the consumer profile

This part is different than metering and billing. This is exposed only to the limited roles in the service chain entity, and each role in the entity may have a different view.

4.1.5 Service Usage and Billing

Usage-based billing is the fundamental consideration of the XaaS model. Typical attributes include:

1. **Metering**—the process of measuring and recording the usage of an entire service, individual parts of a service, or specific services and resources. A service provider may not expose metering information other than the standard billing details accessible to the bill payer. When designing metering systems, the service provider would consider the scenario in which it will operate. The appropriate choices for the metering methods, and the items that are metered, differ based on factors such as business requirements, service type, and the customer or user base.

2. **Billing**—most often a separate and independent function. Usage-based billing may have several billing plans such as:
   a. Pay-per-use plans where customers are billed based on the resources they use. Specific instrumentation must be included in the application to support metering for billing.
   b. Fixed fee plans where customers pay a regular amount that covers

all the vendor's fixed and ongoing costs. One advantage of this plan is that it does not require specific instrumentation to support metering for billing purposes.

   c. Combination plans where there is a fixed monthly fee with additional metered charges based on the usage of specific features, services, or resources. This does require specific instrumentation to be included in the service to support metering for billing.

3. **Instrumentation**—how a service exposes itself for monitoring and measuring. There are different types of instrumentation used for different purpose. Services in the XaaS model have two distinctive purposes: usage measurement for billing and health monitoring for operating. Telemetry is an implied part of the instrumentation, although it is a separate functional part. The process of gathering remote information that is collected by instrumentation is usually referred to as Telemetry. Instrumentation and telemetry, if not designed properly, will place a constraint on billing and maintain the service operationally. Consider the following points when designing an instrumentation and telemetry system:

   a. Identify the combination of information you need to collect. There is no point in collecting information that you will never use.

   b. Segregate instrumentation with the purpose. Instrumentation for usage and billing is entirely different than that for health monitoring and controls.

   c. Consider implementing two (or more) separate channels for telemetry data for different purposes.

   d. Ensure you collect all information you need for the purpose.

   e. Careful categorization of the data when it is written to the data store can simplify analysis.

   f. The mechanisms for collecting and storing the data must themselves be scalable, as the service is.

   g. Where possible, minimize the load on the service by using asynchronous code or queues.

h. Remove old or stale telemetry data that is no longer relevant.

4. Measurement units are important commercial requirements. Complex service billing plans will drive the need for nontraditional measurement units that in turn will drive instrumentation requirements.

4.1.6 Service Monitoring and Control

This is the new avatar of the CI monitoring or discrete component monitoring siloed approach of the legacy technology management practice.

1. Health model: Service health model is the reference state used to benchmark against the real-time model by service monitoring, and take appropriate control action by using the control system. This is of exclusive interest to the service operator, who is responsible for keeping the service operational. The status information is often presented to the consumer through the on-demand portal, just like airlines provide flight status in real time.

2. Instrumentation: As described in the previous section, the instrumentation build for monitoring is different than the instrumentation build for billing.

4.1.7 Self-Service

Self-service is not new either in the IT world or the business world. In fact, the business world has been using technology to implement self-service long before IT did so. Airlines have moved a variety of services into self-service mode throughout the service delivery lifecycle. Self-service components may vary depending upon the type of service. In some cases, manual intervention could be mandatory; for example, in airline self-check-in service for international travel, the intervention of an airline agent is required to check visa validity. The following are a few attributes of self-service:

1. Information service is normally delivered by the knowledge management system that includes a variety of records which enable user to learn using the service correctly to obtain the full value of the service or guided fixing of the issues at the consumer end.

2. User-managed fulfillment is delivered by automation, and examples include software installation, printer configuration, and so on. In the business world, it includes money transfers in banks or seat allocation on airlines.

3. Status tracking of individual service and order tracking of individual orders are other examples of transaction management services.

A service creator would define and publish the self-service component for every service. There are incentives for everyone in the service chain to make as many self-service components as possible. Self -service is a high value component is every catalogued service. Assisted support would be the thing of past very soon. In many cases the assisted support would either not be economically viable or become irrelevant because of self-healing characteristics of the service. Besides this, self-service would be much easy to obtain. We see these examples in airline and personal banking industry. Why it cannot happen in enterprise IT? The new generation workforce prefers self-service anyway. Of course, some form of assisted service would exist but the assistance would be delivered by artificially intelligent machines and not by human.

4.1.8 Service Support

Everything cannot be self-serviceable, or, even if it is, it may fail at some point in time, and recourse to a human service support is a real requirement. The service support role is included in the service chain entity for that purpose. Service support properties of service include:

1. Assisted service—human support service transaction management describes the methods and rules for providing assisted service. Agent-assisted software installation or configuration is an IT example, and a flight change under certain circumstances in the airline service is the business example.

2. Administration of self-service—also part of service support.

A good service support will also diminish the need of complex and expensive user support.

4.1.9 Service Security

Although security is the encompassing, overall function, the specific security attributes are:

1. Access controls

Traditional access controls are very applicable. What may differ is the method of granting the access. The access-granting method is largely technology dependent. For example, the access granting to use a service is different than the granting access to customer to order upgrade on existing service that is related to financial authorization or a commitment to pay.

2. Authentication and authorization

Current practices of authentication and authorization would be applicable as is, but the complexity may grow because of the diversity of the services, service providers, and consumers.

3. Entitlements

Entitlements would be profile-driven and would add complexity. Present day technology allows extreme granular controls. We have seen how airlines change the entitlement based on the passenger profile and the service class.

Information security discipline has been in existence in all enterprises and demonstrating its absolute value (as well as enforcing its nuisance value) but in XaaS world, it will require a new approach. While the security compliance would become even more complex because of access from anywhere, at anytime and from any device is an integral part of the XaaS. Also, to apply security and yet to maintain the user experience is a big challenge. Security professionals need to come out with the mindset of applying security in the context of risk appetite rather than bringing out unilateral security standards.

4.2 XaaS Enablement through Service Architecture

Compliance with the service architecture will ensure that all of the elements of a service are incorporated for delivery in XaaS mode.

Ability to get published in a catalog is ensured by the inclusion of all the elements of the service before it appears in the catalog. The architectural elements would serve as a checklist for the catalog manager to check the completeness. For example:
1. Are the service description and function clearly defined?
2. Are the classification and categorization established for navigation and browsing?
3. Are the consumption components and deliverables clearly defined?
4. Are metering and billing in place?
5. Are self-service components published?
6. Is the service chain entity making a complete link, or is any link broken?

Besides this, the XaaS model is natively designed for cloud deployment that makes services scalable, flexible, virtual, and shared by design.

XaaS service Design versus SaaS Application Design

While we have discussed about service architecture for XaaS, we also want to touch base the complementing topic of application design for XaaS compliance. The XaaS service, in our consideration is essentially a business service and it is produced by the execution of one or more application and delivers a set of benefits. (refer our fundamental definition of service).

These applications can be either cloud enabled or modern cloud-ready web applications, natively designed to run on cloud. In context of XaaS these applications are offered in SaaS model. So, when we talk about XaaS service we are referring to the business service that complies with the XaaS architecture described in this book. However the underlying enablement of XaaS business service comes from the SaaS application that is cloud enabled or natively designed for cloud.

There is a difference between cloud enabled and natively designed for cloud. There are many ways to define cloud native-ness, but we consider the 12 factor app methodology as the defacto standard and criteria to judge the cloud native-ness. The 12 factor app is a software methodology and best practices for building modern, scalable applications. A good reading is available at https://12factor.net on this topic. Such applications are agnostic to the underlying compute layer and can leverage serverless compute service in cloud.

Cloud enablement can be achieved by some enhancement in existing application without the criteria of twelve factor apps. These applications still run in cloud in container or in virtual machines. A business service not natively conceived and designed for XaaS can still be offered as XaaS, similarly applications not natively designed for cloud can be migrated to cloud. Cloud vendors offer both kind of solutions. For example IBM Bluemix OpenWhisk, Amazon Lambada and Azure Function are the offerings for natively designed application for cloud from IBM, Amazon and Microsoft respectively. Similarly IBM Container and IBM OpenStack from IBM, Azure container and Azure VM from Microsoft are offered for cloud enabled applications.

5 Next-Gen Service Management for the XaaS Model

5.1 New Service Management Approach Needed

I n the 21st century, IT is embedded everywhere. I, thus, believe that it would be appropriate to use the term Service Management (SM) rather than IT Service Management (ITSM). It makes me wonder that the industry that claims to adopt and follow the advance trends in technology turns a blind eye in the area of service management and continues to practice decade old legacy systems. Interestingly, the way enterprises do service management is perfectly suited for a world that does not exist.

In this new world, XaaS is the new delivery model, and the industry warrants new approaches to service management. XaaS is a collective term that is said to stand for a number of things, including "X as a service," where X can stand for everything (and anything). This is a rapidly expanding model that grew from a utility service model and is applied to IT and now non-IT services as well. XaaS is the essence of cloud computing, and the most common examples of XaaS are Software as a Service (SaaS), Infrastructure as a Service and Platform as a Service.

In this section, I intend to explain why the IT industry needs to open their eyes and look at the huge gap in the state of the current tools and practices in the service management area.

5.1.1 The Relevance of ITIL

ITIL V2 was released in the year 2001 around the same time as Windows XP. Both were good for that era and environment. While Windows XP is out of support and a dead product, ITIL is still being used across enterprises. I agree that technology changes dynamically. Yet, the approach to deliver and manage the services out of those technologies have not been able to keep the pace with the dynamic technological development. One may argue that ITIL V3 came in 2008, but the truth is that the historical ITIL V2 practices of incident management, change management, and CMDB among others that forms the major practice area in the ITIL implementation still remain the same.

Let's have a look at other disruptions. Where was VMware in 2001? What about cloud? There was no virtualization or cloud then. The enterprise IT infrastructure was monolithic, based on client server architecture. ITIL was primarily designed for an environment that was largely static.

Today's enterprise IT environment is highly virtualized and also moving to cloud. Therefore, the traditional ITIL practices do not make sense. For example, you dynamically move the machine from one host to another using vMotion and also scale up or down node in a cluster using auto scale feature of vRealize, and RFC is totally eliminated. You also do not need several controls prescribed in ITIL for software license compliance because you are consuming SaaS and not buying the license. In other words, the relevance of ITIL is diminishing as rapidly as the monolithic IT infrastructure is shrinking.

However, enterprises are still obsessed with ITIL and applying to the entire infrastructure. I understand the obsession of enterprise with ITIL. But I don't understand why. In a typical ITIL theme, service providers are internal support groups and external service providers. In the XaaS world, this is replaced by service supply chain with new roles such as service creator, service operator, service provider, service broker, and service integrator.

ITIL also was designed with the functional structure of tower-based organization that are serving to business customers. Today in the DevOps world, development, operation and business itself are embedded in one team. In all, ITIL needs radical transformation to meet the requirements of todays' enterprises.

5.1.2 The Generation of Born Digital

There is a dramatic change in the profile of service consumers. We find majority of enterprise users born digital. Traditional customers are being replaced by a new generation of millennials. A large number of users in the enterprise are digital settlers—people who are not born with today's technologies but adopted it very well. These two classes of enterprise users now form the majority, making digital immigrants into minority who are baffled with today's technology and continue to use old way of working. The question is, who are your customers? Often, the responsibility of building and rolling out services is left to the digital immigrants in the organization who see things from their point of view rather than the new generation point of view. We need to understand that today, users demand for the ability to consume service on demand, anytime, from anywhere and from any device and empowerment for a true self service.

5.1.3 User Support Is Out and Service Support Is In.

There is a big difference in user support and service support. In the user support mode, there is no boundary of the service support; support can span across multiple services. In service support mode, the support boundary has a specific warranty and utility. For example, if you have an issue with Internet service, then you call Internet service provider. Similarly, if there is an issue with your desktop/laptop, then you call your equipment seller or you fix it yourself. However, the modern world service is designed for self-service, not human-assisted service. Relying on the user support with helpdesk for user experience is not viable. Take the example of enterprise e-mail service versus Google Gmail service. Typically, an enterprise will produce email service and data center using a cluster of MS exchange servers and AD server form. Of late, it is moved in cloud with office 365, nevertheless the helpdesk support for e-mail is still required. Typically, an enterprise of 50,000 users will have 4-5 persons on service desk to support e-mail, attachment and OneDrive-related issue. On one hand, there will be restrictions on what device can be used to consume the service. On the other hand, we've got Gmail (and Google drive) that has a user base of 1 billion, anytime service, anywhere on any device without any restrictions and with absolutely no service desk, and still the user experience is far superior. The most important difference is that Google has built the service for user experience by design, not by relying on assisted support.

5.1.4 Service Catalog becomes The Core Of SM

In the ITIL world, CMDB was the center of the ITSM universe around which everything revolved. The theme was that the service is produced by Configuration Item (application CI, server CI, and database CI to name a few). Since CI is related to another CI, we need CMDB to understand and manage the service. In the modern world, a service is essential in a XaaS model and is composed of micro services, and each micro service is independent. CMDB is now deep below in the value chain. While service catalog has come on the top of the value chain. ITIL promoted the idea of CMDB in the year 2002 and as we mentioned in the first section, it has become outdated now. In the era of XaaS, service is composed by micro services and each micro service is independent. Service catalog brings in standardization and quality. If a service is published in the catalog, it is available according to the specifications published. You cannot ask for your own specifications or requirement. You can personalize service as much as a service provider allows. So, the customization is out and personalization is in.

5.1.5 Crowdsourcing Is The Key

The ubiquity of networked people inside and outside enterprises has changed the collaboration and communication radically. The 'mobile population' is debating, discussing, and collaborating all the time thru channels within and outside the enterprise. One very good illustration will be the use of crowd sourcing for knowledge management. Enterprises are spending a lot of money on building the knowledge base for the IT support. A typical knowledge-management system includes processes to source, verify, authorize and publish. The typical roles include knowledge contributor, SME, technical writer and knowledge manager. The processes and the roles guarantee the correctness of the knowledge record. In most cases, it's the wastage of money because investments are not made in maintaining the currency of knowledge, and thus the knowledge base becomes irrelevant quickly. However, the user is most of the time tempted to google the problem and look for solution on the Internet rather than using The ubiquity of networked people inside and outside enterprises has changed the collaboration and communication radically. The 'mobile population' is debating, discussing, and collaborating all the time thru channels within and outside the enterprise. One very good illustration will be the use of crowd sourcing for knowledge management. Enterprises are spending a lot of money on building the knowledge base for the IT support. A typical knowledge-management system includes processes to source, verify, authorize and publish. The typical roles include knowledge contributor, SME, technical writer and knowledge manager. The processes and the roles guarantee the correctness of the knowledge record. In most cases, it's the wastage of money because investments are not made in maintaining the currency of knowledge, and thus the knowledge base becomes irrelevant quickly. However, the user is most of the time tempted to google the problem and look for solution on the Internet rather than using

5.2 Approach for Next Gen Service management

So, what should be the next generation service-management system? There's many considerations available. However, I would like to emphasize a few highly relevant considerations.while it is actually the performance of the 'fulfilment service'. It fits very well into the fundamental definition of a service — benefits produced by execution of activities.

5.2.1 Start From Service Catalog

If service catalog is the center of SM universe, the new generation of service-management system should be built on the foundation of service catalog. In order to build a true service catalog, service architecture becomes very critical. We see a large number of diversified services. Traditional relational database management system cannot support diversified service structure. Therefore, unstructured database or non-relational database becomes necessary. Classic IT service catalogs are actually 'Request Item' catalogs (or Service Request catalogs). They are primarily designed for initiating a transaction-based service and the fulfilment of a specific item for the requestor. A typical Service Request Management System (SRMS) will generate a task or work order, automate the workflow to deal with that order, and the finally fulfilment happens manually. The same SRMS is also positioned as a self-service implementation tool, both by the vendors and the IT organization. The ability of the user to go to the portal, submit and track the request as it progresses is deemed as the self-service element. This is a long way from achieving real self-service—in classic SRMS implementation models, a true service catalog element and a true self-service element are typically missing.

The most common example of self-service is service support in password reset automation. In the case of service delivery scenarios, a cloud service provisioning process is another common example. Service delivery systems may also allow you to provision, start, stop and reboot your service. We find frequent examples in the business world. For example, personal banking services allow you to pay bills and transfer money, or with automated airline services, yo can book a new flight or change the seat without the provider's intervention.

Is an 'item' in the request catalog a service? Classical SRMS systems publish a catalog of 'item' to be delivered. SRMS generates a task (work order) and relies on the execution of the task to deliver the service. In fact, an item published in the request catalog may or may not be a service. A physical item or product, though not a service, can be deemed as one – because the execution of the task delivers the physical item (say a laptop) while it is actually the performance of 'fulfilment service'. It fits very well into the fundamental definition of a service — benefits produced by execution of activities.

What about non-tangible items that really are services? Tasks are generated for fulfilment, but does the execution of the task actually produce the desired service? A classic request catalog may not have the mechanism necessary to guarantee that in the fulfilment process and may even require external systems processes. This is very likely to happen if the fulfilment tasks are manually performed.

In other words, the item in the catalog may fail the criteria of being a service. A service in the service catalog may be composed of multiple services – requiring orchestration across multiple service providers for delivery fulfilment. Such examples are common across businesses including travel services; travel companies, for instance, offer airline, hotel, and car-rental bookings among others.

In IT operations, especially in XaaS models such as PaaS and SaaS, provisioning processes require orchestration across multiple elements. The XaaS era will herald a new avatar of the service catalog that will incorporate orchestration as an integral element of the service catalog. A XaaS system would publish the consumption component, and the integrated orchestration model would be used for seamless outcome fulfilment and delivery – the entire process visible in the catalog.

5.2.2 Catalog Aggregation & Service Orchestration

In the era of service proliferations, the demand for service cannot be fulfilled by a single service provider, and thus market is wide open for multiple service providers. With the surging demand of services, the number of service providers is also increasing fast. Each service provider focuses on niche services. Therefore, a role of catalog aggregation has emerged. With the proliferation of service providers, it will not be viable to build and publish the service catalog, and thus catalog aggregation will be the only option. Aggregated catalog will have multiple service creators. Therefore, service orchestration will automatically become a mandatory requirement. Service orchestration is the new generation of operation integration part of SIAM, which is popular in the multiple managed service provider scenario. Why enterprise IT is struggling to publish a service catalog of 400 items (an average number of items in an enterprise IT) for a user base of less than 50,000 (average number, again), while Amazon.com is successfully publishing and maintaining a catalog of 12 million items for a 244 million user base. And that is not all. Amazon is also successfully delivering all orders originating from that catalog. Let's have a look at this case, in detail.

5.2.3 It Is Build Vs. Aggregate.

Amazon is not really building and publishing the catalog. It is actually aggregating catalogs – an important difference in the approach as against the traditional legacy practice of building a catalog on your own. There are thousands of supplier catalogs beneath the system that are not visible to buyers. Amazon itself is one of those suppliers. In other words, catalog building and maintenance is virtually outsourced. However, the main success lies in designing a catalog model and structure. In addition, the UX and UI of the IT service catalog are also essential to accommodate vast and diversified product categories.

5.2.4 It Is Fulfilling Vs. Orchestrating

Catalog aggregation is only a part of the business. One cannot make money unless the orders are delivered. The Amazon approach is unique in this area; it does not deliver the packages but orchestrates the delivery from the suppliers. The reason behind the success of such a model lies in clearly defined policies for the supply chain and interfacing points.

Can Enterprises Replicate Amazon's Model? Yes, they can. In fact, replication of the above model is not difficult for enterprise IT, if the CIOs are willing to adopt it. It's not easy, but it's worth the effort. However, the typical challenges, which may come along the way are:

1. Tool/Platform: Traditional ITIL-based tools are conditioning implementers, devised to design and publish 'form-based' catalog items. One has to adopt service-architecture based approach, which will establish a single generic model and structure across all services. It will also standardize the IT service catalog structure. Adopt service-architecture based approach, which will establish a single generic model and structure.

2. Organizational Culture: Individual technology tower has to come out of the technology management mindset and think of itself as part of the service supply chain, which is either creating a service or delivering it.

5.2.5 Think Of Self-service

What is a true self-service element? True self-service allows you to obtain the outcome without any intervention from service providers. If you have to await the execution of the fulfilment task by the provider, after having submitted a request for a service, then it is not known as true self-service.

In traditional ITSM tools' service catalog, you are able to track the task's progress as the service provider staff is working on the tasks. However, the outcome is not obtained, andtherefore the ability to track progress is also not a true self-service element. True self-service can be realized by appropriate service design, automation and empowering the service consumer with the ability to run the automated fulfilment method.

The XaaS world will usher in a new avatar of self-service. We envision a dedicated database to maintain the self-service component for each service and IT service management tool. A service may have multiple self-service components – each self-service component designed for a specific task. These tasks are either automated through API, or they invoke an orchestration model (execution method). Information about all of the above elements together forms a self-service delivery database.

5.2.6 Think Of BOYD & Mobility

Let us look at how born digital generation is consuming the services in their personal life. Personal banking services like bill payment, money transfer and such are consumed using laptop/desktop or mobile device of the consumer choice. Bank does not dictate, which device to use for consuming its services. So, does the Internet service provider or the telecomm service provider. Then why enterprise should dictate the stands of the service consuming end points? It is time for enterprise to think of BYOD and not enforcing the standard devices upon users.

5.2.7 Think Of Entitlement-based Delivery

Form and field based catalog are workflow-based services where a requestor submits a request that goes through the approval process, and then fulfillment happens. In the era of XaaS, the service is standardized and relies on the entitlement logic. Every consumer has a user profile and every service has a service profile. A combination of these two profiles can very well determine the entitlement and delivery. It is assumed that every service is standard, and there is no scope of customization. This would be a cultural change in the enterprise, but we believe that the new generation is very well accustomed to standardization and entitlement.

5.2.8 Think Of Nirvana State

Every enterprise has a datacenter. Think of this as a IT service production factory. Servers, databases, and applications are the machinery to manufacture the IT service that is delivered by network pipeline to the end devices. Since the early era of MIS (1980's), the tradition in all enterprises has been to build the in-house service producing factory. CIOs have employed large number of staff whose mind set is to maintain the machinery rather than producing service.

In nirvana state, CIOs will demolish all the factory and quit the role of service producer. In this state, CIO will run an orchestration platform rather than a factory. In this platform, he will plug in diversified service creators along with entities in service supply chain roles (service operator, integrator, and broker among others). Each service creator will come with his own catalog and CIO will merely aggregate and orchestrate the fulfillment. So, CIO would quit the role of service producer and take the role of service orchestrator. Let me illustrate with a hypothetical scenario. E-mail service and personal storage service are the most essential services in any organization. Instead of producing these service in the datacenter, CIO can plug in multiple service providers such as Microsoft mail, MS OneDrive, Google Mail, Google Drive, Dropbox and yahoo mail, and aggregate the catalog and let the service consumer choose what he/she wants.

Achieving the nirvana state is not easy, but the proliferation of Cloud and XaaS model is creating an environment to achieve that state. So, along with the technology roadmap, it is essential to establish a commensurate roadmap for new generation of service management. It is also a cultural shift, but keeping in mind the characteristic of born digital users, the market will move in that direction. CIO has to choose from - adopt or get irrelevant.

5.3 The Role Of SCDB

The fundamental concept behind CMDB was that the 'service is produced by CIs'. The IT infrastructure was almost static, and it was important to know the impact of any change in a CI within the static infrastructure. However, the premise in the XaaS world is that the 'service is composed by micro services' and the infrastructure is dynamically changing. Therefore, it is SCDB (Service Composition Database) now, that replaces CMDB in the XaaS environment.

The paradigms of the XaaS world lead towards the concept of SCDB – *Service Composition Database (SCDB)*, the equivalent of CMDB in XaaS world.

CMDB (Configuration Management Database)	SCDB (Service Composition Database)
CMDB is the database of CIs and their relationships that produce a service	SCDB is the database of microservices and their relationship with a service
CI is a part of ICT Infrastructure that need to me managed individually as well as collectively	Microservice is independent service focused on specific function/outcome exposed through API and need to be managed individually
CMDB deals with CI Classes and CI Attributes with relationship types for CI to CI relationship	SCDB deals with Microservice classes and service properties – Microservice to microservice relationship not applicable
CMDB is n:n relation between CIs and in multitier CI hierarchy it is overwhelming complex	SCDB is 1:n relation between service and microservice and in multitier hierarchy it is relatively simple
XSMDB	

Therefore, we would need SCDB in XaaS service management as much as we needed CMDB in ITIL world. Typical enterprise landscape is hybrid that includes classic IT and cloud based IT, hence CMDB as well as SCDB both needed to address different kinds of needs. As the "As a Service Model" and cloud adoption rise, the scope of CMDB would decline. Therefore, we bring in the concept of XSMDB – XaaS service Management Database. XSMDB has two parts

- SCDB- Service Composition Database – To support the management of applications designed with microservice architecture
- CMDB- Configuration Management Database- To support the legacy monolithic application designed in client server architecture

What should be the structure of XSMDB?

Given that the contemporary enterprise IT would consist of the hybrid environment that includes

1. XaaS model enabled by natively designed cloud applications in containers in cloud
2. XaaS model enabled by natively designed cloud applications in containers in enterprise private cloud
3. XaaS/traditional service supported by cloud enabled applications running on managed IaaS Cloud
4. Legacy applications running in unmanaged IaaS cloud
5. Legacy application in legacy infrastructure

When you drill down a service into microservice and further; you will have touch points with in-house infrastructure as well as cloud and would. Thus, a drilldown of SCDB will have a touchpoint with CMDB.

I believe that XSMDB should be formed with two distinctive database technologies. Traditional CMDB in *Graph database* that would eliminate the need of external service mapping tools. It should not include non-discoverable data (owner, supporter etc.) would be a part of Catalog and portfolio. Other the other hand SCDB should be built in *NOSQL database* and service Properties derived from service architecture.

6 XaaS System Architecture

The purpose of this section is to present a hypothetical system suitable for the XaaS service management. We firmly believe in the need for such a system now, and, looking forward in the market, some future-looking vendor will think in this direction to build and offer such a system.

6.1 Overview

Figure 8 is the functional architecture of the system that presents the key functional blocks and how they are connected with each other.

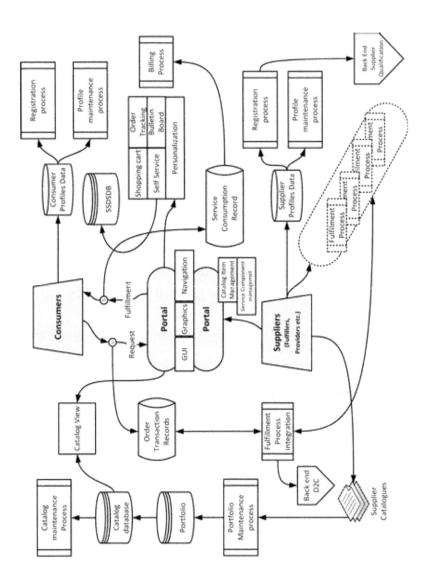

Figure 8: Functional architecture of XaaS system

At the center, we have a service portal that presents the catalog to the consumer through which a consumer can initiate service requests. Portfolio Management and Catalog Management is essential parts to control the service-offering pipeline. Fulfillment can happen through an external system.

6.2 Important Functional Components

6.2.1 Portal

Portal forms a one-stop shop for the enterprise users for shopping IT and business services. It aggregates various underlying catalogs to provide a unified experience to its users for requesting services. The portal typically consists of the following functionalities:

1. Catalog aggregation
2. Shopping like experience to service consumers
3. Automated fulfillment through orchestration of various fulfillment systems
4. Shopping-like experience to users
5. Tracking of service requests for clear visibility (users can track the fulfillment status with expected dates)
6. Notifications of various lifecycle stages of a request for a service
7. Integrated survey mechanism for instant feedback on quality of service provided
8. Approval mechanism for requests raised
9. Access to latest news and other updates with audio and video content
10. Guidance available in form of online help
11. Solicit support through chat, e-mail, or phone
12. Self-help and knowledge articles

Design for User Experience

One of the critical aspects of the portal is user-experience-based service design, and it would be worthwhile to cite the example of Apple 3D touch.

iPhone 6 introduces an entirely new way to interact with your phone. In addition to familiar multi-touch gestures such as tap, swipe, and pinch, iPhone can now sense the amount of pressure applied to the display, which brings a new dimension of functionality to the iPhone experience.

When you use 3D Touch, iPhone responds with subtle taps enabling the user not only see the outcome but feel it too; thus enhancing the overall user experience. 3D Touch is one of the most innovative features to appear on a mobile phone touchscreen since pinch to zoom, swiping, and other actions we all now take for granted. 3D Touch isn't just a new feature that Apple has tacked on to its phone; it's a fundamental change to the way users interact with their iPhone.

When you start with user experience, 3D touch starts with an idea of detecting force on a thin device. While, from a traditional designer perspective, it would be a matter of designing to detect a force, detecting the force would fail to deliver the experience because a user's experience is not just related to force on a device.

A designer from a user-experience perspective will not think of a design to detect the force but design to sense the intent of the user. Here, the designer is trying to read minds. And there is a user who might be using his or her thumb or finger: he or she may be emotional at the moment, and he or she may be walking or just relaxing on a couch. All of these scenarios do not affect the intent, but they do affect what a sensor inside the thin iPhone 6 sees.

So there are huge design challenges and corresponding challenges in capturing intent that lead to huge amounts of complexity in the components' design as well. Here, a sensor cannot be a simple transducer. It should be combined with an accelerometer to nullify the effect of gravity. Again, nullifying may mean adding or subtracting the force depending upon the direction of the motion. Similarly, the difference of thumb and finger is important to interpret the force. So Apple fused an accelerometer in the sensor to detect the nature of interaction and added algorithms. This was one of the basic things, and if they didn't get it right, nothing that is built upon it would work. Apple did it right and stood apart from all competition, maintaining its innovative lead.

While the portal design and GUI provides the first interaction and experience of using the service, the design of GUI is not the only user-experience part; in the experience with the real service that the user is consuming via portal (or mobile application), the complexity is even higher. If a mobile telecomm service provider has a great self-service portal (a great mobile app to use that), it would still not help if the voice quality of the telecom service were poor. To bring in a great user experience, a service designer must defy the fundamental rule of psychology that states, "we see things not as they are but as we are"; and learn to see things as the user sees them. Although this is not easy, there are design principles to design a service for user experience, and those are totally nontechnical. Unfortunately, enterprise IT is largely infected by the tendency of solving every problem with technology, and if this tendency continues, it will multiply the challenge. I see the external business world now forcing enterprise IT to think differently, and that is a positive sign.

6.2.2 Consumer Profile Management

In all traditional service management systems, we do have the user profile management concept. Consumer profile management is almost the same except that the attributes in the profile go much beyond those maintained in the user profile data. A consumer profile is used for marketing and advertising purposes. Market segments are created and identified by the consumer profiles and differentiated on parameters like:

- Demographic: attributes related to age, city or region of residence, gender, race and ethnicity, and composition of household
- Brand affinity/product usage: attributes associated with product engagement on the basis of behavior
- Generation: attributes related to a specific, identifiable generation cohort group
- Geography: attributes related to a specific, identifiable generation cohort group
- Geodemographics: attributes that combine geography and

demographics, which may cluster into an identifiable group

- Benefits sought: attributes related to the benefits that consumers seek when they shop for products and services

Market researchers may develop proprietary consumer profiles, or they may use panels of consumers who have been classified according to their common attributes. Market research provider firms often make their consumer profiles available for discrete market research projects that are conducted for their market research clients at large companies.

6.2.3 SSDSDB (Self-Service Delivery and Support Database)

We envision a dedicated database to maintain the self-service component for each service. A service may have multiple self-service components. Each self-service component is designed to do a specific task. These tasks are automated through API or invoke some kind of orchestration (execution method). Information about all of the above forms a self-service delivery database. For example, here is a table showing a simple SSDSDB.

Service Name	IaaS (Infrastructure as a Service)				
Consumption Component	Windows Virtual Machine				
Self-Service Item	Input/ Trigger	Execution Method	Outcome	Cycle Time	Notification
Reboot machine	User click	Script	Server rebooted	3 minutes	Successful reboot
Add memory	Price acceptance click	API	Memory provisioning	45 secs	Successful upgrade
Service Name	Office 365				
Consumption Component	Personal storage anywhere (one drive)				
Self-Service Item	Input/ Trigger	Execution Method	Outcome	Cycle Time	Notification
Increase Storage Quota	Price acceptance click	API	Storage allocation resize	45 secs	Successful upgrade

Table 2: SSDSDB illustration

In a real system, we envision a comprehensive table that will include other fields such as entitlement, validation rules, prerequisites, user-interface controls, and so on. We see the business examples on a daily basis; service provider for our cell phones offers many self-service components, though we do not have insight on how those individual actionable records are maintained. Also, it is not necessary to have a predefined schema for SSDSDB because every service will have a unique self-service record, and the same schema will not apply to every service.

6.2.4 Portfolio and Catalog

The service portfolio contains current services being offered, proposed services, and retired services. The service portfolio is divided into three sections: service pipeline, service catalog, and retired services.

- Service pipeline is the list of proposed services but currently not available for consumption
- Service catalog is the list of services currently being offered for consumption
- Retired services is the list of that are withdrawn and no longer available for consumption.

Services should be clustered according to lines of service based on common business activities they support. Only active services are visible to customers.

Catalogs represent the consumption component of services listed in a portfolio. For example:
- IaaS is a service; VM is a consumption component.
- E-mail is a service; mailbox/account is a consumption component.

A service can have more than one consumption component. A service can have more than one service, and each service can have one or more consumption components. Catalog items and subscriptions are the consumption component. It may be referred to as an "offering" also.

6.2.5 Fulfillment

Service fulfillment could be either a one-time delivery or a perpetual delivery. Some services may have both. For example, IaaS service will start with a one-time provision of a virtual machine and then an ongoing run of the virtual machine. Similarly, e-mail service will invoke a one-time account creation and then subsequent message transmission reception service. In our service architecture, both components are individually listed and can be independently fulfilled. Each component will have predefined fulfillment processes and roles mapped to a specific entity in the service chain.

New avatar of Service Catalog and self-service

Since the proliferation of ITIL based IT service management tools, many enterprises that have deployed those tools are self complacent to believe that they have brought in the service catalog and self-service. This complacency is actually driven by the tool vendors' definition of service catalog and self-service. While it was good for the purpose during old times, a serious revaluation is required to determine how good is it for the purpose in the new era – the XaaS era.

Classic IT service catalogs are actually a "Request Item" catalogs (or Service Request catalog). They are primarily designed for originating a transaction based service and fulfillment of specific item to the requestor. Typical SR management system will generate a task or work order, automate the workflow to deal with that order and the fulfillment will happen manually. The same SRMS is also positioned as the self-service implementation. The element of self-service is defined as the ability of user to go to the portal, submit request and track the request as it progresses. A true service catalog element and a true self-service element are missing in classic SRMS implementation.

What is a true self-service?

A true self-service allows you to obtain the outcome without service providers' interventions. When you have submitted a request for a service and awaiting the execution of fulfillment task by the provider then it is not a true self-service. You are able to track the progress but the outcome is not reached so ability to track the progress is also not a true self-service. A true self self-service can be realized by appropriate service design and automation and extending the ability to run the automation to the service consumer. Most common example of a self-service is service support is automation of password reset. In service delivery scenarios- a cloud service provisioning is the most common example. Service delivery system allows you to provision, start, stop, and reboot your service. Or in personal banking service you can pay the bill and transfer money, or in airline you can change the flight or change the seat.

XaaS world will bring in a new avatar of self-service. We envision a dedicated database to maintain the self-service component for each service. A service may have multiple self-service components. Each self-service component is designed to do a specific task. These tasks are automated through API or invoke some kind of orchestration (execution method). Information about all of the above forms a self-service delivery database.

Is Item in the Request catalog a service?

SRMS generates a task (work order) and relies on the execution of task to deliver the service. An item published in the request catalog may or may not be a service. A physical item or product though is not a service, but it can be deemed as the service because the execution of the task delivers the physical item (say a laptop) and it is actually the performance of "fulfillment service". It fits very well into the fundamental definition of a service- benefits produced by execution of activities. What about not tangible items that are really a service? Tasks are generated for the fulfillment but does the execution of task actually produce the desired service? Classic request catalog may not have mechanism to guarantee that in the fulfillment process and may require external systems or external process. This is very likely to happen if the fulfillment tasks are manually performed. In other words the item in the catalog may fail on the criteria of being a service. A service in the service catalog may be composed of multiple services and requires orchestration across multiple service providers for delivery/fulfillment. We see these examples in business all the time. Travel service for example offers airline, hotel and car rental booking. In IT operations, especially in XaaS model like PaaS and SaaS provisioning require orchestration across multiple elements.

XaaS world will bring in new avatar of service catalog that will publish the consumption component and integrated orchestration to fulfill and deliver the outcome seamlessly to the consumer and that will be visible in the catalog.

New avatar of knowledge management in self-service systems

In some cases knowledge management is a part of self-service system and it allows users access to the approved knowledge articles, which, in turn enable user to fix the issue. A comprehensive knowledge management process that has multiple roles controls the classical knowledge management system. Typical roles are

1. Knowledge contributor who contributed the data or information that can be processed to form knowledge

2. SME (Subject Matter Expert) who converts the data and information into a valid and authenticated knowledge record

3. Tech writer who packages the knowledge into a form that can easily be consumed

4. Knowledge manager who ensures that the knowledge is current and is being used and the who knowledge management system is working as desired

5. Knowledge consumer – the end user for whom the entire system is designed.

In this system, when a consumer is using some knowledge article, he is assured of the correctness and applicability of the knowledge record.

In the new avatar of knowledge management, the social engineering will take the center stage roles. Traditional roles will just vanish. Crowd sourcing would become the primary theme. Crowd would be the knowledge contributor; crowds would be the knowledge consumer. SME and tech writer roles would become irrelevant and knowledge manager role would be completely automated. The consumer would not have assurance of the correctness and the applicability of the knowledge record.

Trail and error method would be very common and acceptable approach to achieve the end result.

Crowd sourcing is very well working in all home IT infrastructure where we are fixing many issues by trail and error with Google as the crowd sourcing knowledge base.

6.2.6 Data Stores

In our earlier publication, for a traditional ITSM system, we defined ten different kinds of data stores, namely:

1. Service support transactions
2. Service delivery management
3. Capacity Management Information System (CMIS)
4. Availability Management Information System (AMIS)
5. Knowledge Management (KM)
6. Event management Managed Object (MO) data
7. Customer and location
8. Employees and organization
9. Service portfolio and catalog
10. Asset and Configuration Management Database

We envision radical changes in the data stores for the following reasons:

1. Service classes will be so diversified that a standard relational database with predefined schema will not be able to define all of the services. Data stores for the XaaS system will be largely non-relational databases and/or follow schema on-the-fly approach.

2. Graph databases will also step in to meet the new requirements of service maps

3. Unlike the traditional service management system, where all the data

stores are placed in the core system, the need for a centralized approach will be eliminated. Different data sets will have different stakeholders in the service chain; for example, AMIS and CMIS have no use for the orchestrator or integrator role. Hence, the data stores will be distributed and will form a limited federation. Service Catalog and portfolio will be the core databases that are more likely to be non-relational. Customer database would be replaced by consumer profile database. KM will be a subset in SSDSDB.

6.2.7 Detection to Correction

Detect to Correct (D2C) Value Stream is focused on keeping services running in production. D2C provides a framework for integrating monitoring, management, remediation, and other operational aspects. D2C is defined in the IT4IT reference architecture of Open Group. It maps with a series of ITIL processes that include event, incident, problem, and change.

6.2.8 Service Chain Entity Qualification

Portfolio manager qualifies a service, and, after verification, it is published by the catalog manager. In the back end, in addition to the service qualification, a service creator and all the entities in the service chain must also be qualified so that those entities are in good business standing. This maps with the vendor management process in traditional service management.

6.3 Technology for User Experience

User experience is extremely important and perhaps the only factor that will assure business success, yet it is overhyped as some newest mantra. Actually, it is not at all a new mantra and has been very much in focus since Help Desk Institute started to promote the SPOC idea in the late 1990s. This section provides our views on user experience.

Recently, Gartner published a list of technologies that help improve and support customer experiences. Gartner has an exceptional track record of recognizing, formulating, and communicating trailing indicators in the IT industry and this is just one of them. Credit goes to Gartner for the presentation and marketing skills to present old wine in a new bottle. Gartner is very good at this kind of stuff that makes IT-savvy people admire the latest hype cycle curve, and it excites them to search for their favorite company on the latest Magic Quadrant.

Gartner divides customer experience efforts into seven types. These are: listen, think, and do (such as collecting feedback); from out to in (changing processes, customer journey mapping, and finding moments of truth); act as one (being consistent across the organization); open up (demonstrating trust, co-creation); get personal (personalizing products, customizing offers); alter attitudes (empowering employees, governance, and policy); and design better (executing brand, executive strategy, and user-experience design). Based on these factors, Gartner's top ten customer experience (CX) technologies are listed below with our views on each of them.

1. Voice of the customer: A variety of customer survey and feedback systems have been in place for a long time. Old-generation ITSM tools have had incident-driven survey capabilities since the year 2003, to my knowledge. In our first publication, "Process Excellence for IT Operations," we discussed CSAT best practice and how to interpret customer feedback on surveys.

2. Business process management: This is a very old concept and practice. Although, in the IT world, it did not get the importance it deserves (and now the pressure is on IT to accord it its due importance), that does not make this a new part of the digital world. In our first publication, we give a strong emphasis on process management and compare it with software lifecycle management.

3. Multichannel customer service: Even in the old ITSM system, multichannel customer contact is a well-adopted practice that keeps pace with the available technology. E-mail and phones were the primary channels, but over a period of time, more channels such as chat and portals have been added.

4. Customer Analytics: BI systems have been in use for a long time. IT people have ignored it the way they did BPM—and, again, they will not be able to ignore it anymore.

5. Master data management: MDM has been always of importance and repositioning the same old practice in the name of CX technology does not imply that a new discovery has been made.

6. Content management has been in practice since the first generation of websites started appearing in the mid-1990s.

7. Personalization: a well-known feature of every service management system and in practice for over ten years.

8. User-experience design tools and platforms: Since the client server era, GUI design has been regarded as a specialized skill and discipline.

9. Loyalty management: IT is accustomed to a captive customer and so is ignorant about loyalty management, but businesses such as airlines and hotels have had this practice for a long, long time.

10. Privacy management: A privacy setting is common in all collaboration sites and also in applications.

Finally, it is important to note that technology does not create user experience in the same way that technology does not create knowledge in knowledge management solutions or social media does not create social intelligence.

Art and Science of User Experience

Delivering a good user experience is an art because it is an application of human creative skills and it is also science since it is a systematic and logical body of knowledge. This is what we said in the context of customer satisfaction, and it can be repeated for user experience in service management. User experience and customer satisfaction are two different things. The first difference is the party involved. A consumer is different than a bill-payer, though both the roles can be played by the same person also. Second, the experience is the impression and feeling during the occurrence of the event, while the satisfaction is the outcome of the experience.

User experience comes into existence because of user interactions with a person or system during the service consumption. A service consumption can be a specific service transaction of a finite and limited duration, or it could be perpetual, or both. For example, obtaining an incident resolution service, you may interact with an agent or log in to the self-service portal, troubleshoot it, and fix it yourself. This would be a service transaction. However, using an Internet service would be a perpetual service consumption experience. It is a good strategy to rely on the design & build quality of service for user experience rather than relying on support services to deliver the user experience.

In transactional service, the user experience is derived from the channel of interaction, and typical nontechnical elements are screen layouts, including color schemes, GUI, and navigation for system interaction as well as interpersonal qualities such as courtesy and attitude of the human at the provider end. Both require more artistic approaches than the scientific approach because they often do not meet the basic requirements to be considered science: clear quantifiability, highly controlled experimental conditions, reproducibility, predictability, and testability.

Of course, there are technical elements also, such as communication channel quality (voice, network speed, and so on), and functional elements such as the business processes that can be managed scientifically.

In transactional service, the experience is attached to a one-time transaction, and it is transaction-specific and does not change with time after the closure of the transaction. Also, service warranty (fit for use) and service utility (fit for purpose) criteria are applied to the delivered product.

Perpetual service has a different paradigm of user experience. It is derived from that actual service quality that can be managed and governed scientifically. This is the science of user experience. This comes by the design of service. The service warranty (fit for use) and service utility (fit for purpose) are the elements contributing to the user experience in perpetual service consumption and are continually applied to the benefit or the outcome. User experience can dynamically vary with time during the service consumption period. For example, you can be unhappy with Internet service while it is slowed down and happy again as soon as the performance is restored.

Design for user experience also requires nontechnical criteria; we have mentioned this with the illustration of Apple's 3D Touch.

Mind-set of the Service Provider/Creator for User Experience

The impact of the mind-set of a service provider on the user experience can be illustrated by two examples, both coming from the airline industry, which I consider as the role model for a mature service industry.

We are all well acquainted with the term "flight attendant." This role is an essential customer-facing role on every flight. I do not remember when this terminology replaced the old terminology of "flight steward," but it is not just the words that have changed. It is the change of mind-set. "Steward" implies that the person looks after, takes care of, and serves the passengers. The primary criterion of the steward is customer care. A flight attendant is now concerned with safety and security compliance and policing the guidelines for safety and security. The primary criterion of taking care of customer is just gone in the background. You can very well relate how the approach has deteriorated the passenger experience.

Automation and technology deployment approach is not sufficient for providing a good customer experience. Despite the automation and advanced technology deployment, the flight times between heavily traveled routes have actually increased over the last forty years. Here is the actual data (from departedflights.com):

New York JFK to Boston Logan from forty-seven minutes to seventy-four minutes (57 percent increase)
Detroit DTW to Miami from 150 minutes to 178 minutes (18 percent increase)
Los Angeles LAX to San Francisco from thirty-three minutes to fifty-one minutes (54 percent increase)
Atlanta ATL to San Francisco from 293 minutes to 325 minutes (11 percent increase)

Of course, increased traffic is one of the factors, but it is not the only factor. Airlines have changed the criterion from saving time to saving fuel. (Flying faster burns more fuel.) Also, the fuel efficiency also impacts the maintenance of a comfortable cabin temperature. The flight duration and cabin temperature both have a direct impact on the passenger experience. Like wise in IT, even though the CPU power is growing dramatically, the memory size of the system is growing rapidly, the network bandwidth is growing also but correspondingly the file size and media files and applications are also getting resource hungry.

Even in the product design, mind set of designer impacts the experience. European car manufactures first thinks of the car quality standards and then work backward to realize those standards in the minimum price point. American car manufactures, start with a price point and then work backward to deliver the best quality in that price point. And we do know the user experience while driving a European car and an American car.

7 Service Lifecycle Management

A typical lifecycle could spread across the service value chain, and each entity in the value chain could be a different enterprise. For example, service design may be completely mapped to service creator, but the service operation is fully mapped to the service provider. That means the processes, as defined in contemporary frameworks such as ITIL, COBIT, and IT4IT, need some adjustment.

7.1 Building and Deployment

Building and deployment starts with service creation. In a traditional enterprise ITSM environment, it starts from strategy. Open groups' IT4IT reference architecture suggests the beginning point in the value chain as Strategy-to-Portfolio (S2P). This value stream focuses on building the portfolio on the basis of the strategy. The next value stream is Requirement-to-Deploy (R2D) that focuses on deploying or publishing actually useable service into the catalog. From the practical implementation perspective of the SaaS model, the service creation strategy and building may be completely outside enterprise IT and under the control of a niche service creator. So we will merge S2P and R2D into a single process that will cover from building to deployment. Here, we envision two scenarios. The first scenario is about the market pull, where service consumers are raising demands for new or enhanced services, and the creator creates those services on a reactive basis. In the second scenario, a service creator may create, a new service proactively and assume all the risk of investment in creating the service because he or she is sure of the business proposition and then takes it to the market.

From a practical "process" implementation point of view, we suggest merging of S2P and R2D of IT4IT reference architecture and making it "Demand-to-Deployment process" for simplification.

7.1.1 Market Pull

Based on the business forecast or to compete with competitors, business demands the type of service that suits the market condition. Demands come from business through strategic decision. Businesses communicate the need to portfolio managers so that services will be created to meet their requirements. Portfolio managers analyze these needs, identify and consult with creators, and provide the end-to-end lifecycle of the service.

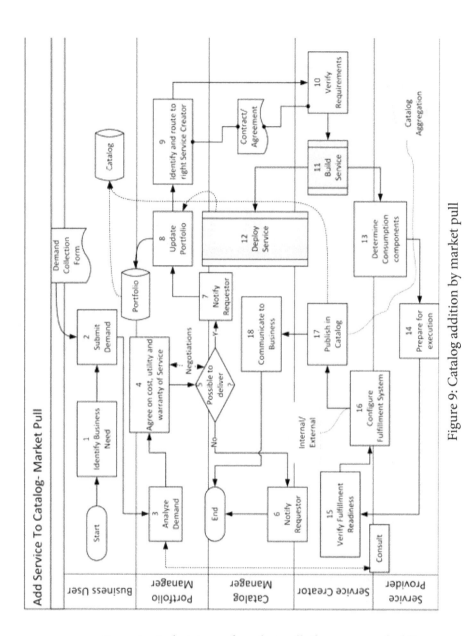

Figure 9: Catalog addition by market pull

we are presenting a typical picture of market pull, the process of adding a service to the catalog. Five roles participate in this process—namely, business user, portfolio manager, catalog manager, service creator, and service provider. The trigger comes from the business user, who identifies business needs and provides specific business requirements in the form of business demands. That means, within this process, there should be a well-defined sub-process and structure, including templates to collect the demand. This is very similar to traditional ITSM demand management. Open group IT4IT reference architecture provides a good guidance on this, including data objects. A portfolio manager analyzes a demand, and, in this analysis, he or she will consult a service provider and service creator to ensure that such a demand fulfillment is technically viable. In this consultation, he or she will also come up with a cost estimate to create and operate such a service. He or she will then negotiate with the business user again, especially on cost, utility, and warranty of services. During this negotiation, the service provider and service creator are also likely to be consulted. This will go into multiple iterations. At the end of this negotiation, there will be a clear decision whether the service is going to make its way into the catalog or not. If the decision is made to build and publish the service, then the portfolio is updated, and responsibility of building the service is handed over to the service creator. Depending upon the enterprise policy, there may be additional contract negotiation with the service creator.

Once the creator has built it, the service creator will also define consumption components and offering. Under the control of the catalog manager, it will be published and communicated to the business. Several architectural compliance checklists can be enforced at the time of publishing. This includes:

1. Configuring the fulfillment system with the fulfilling entity.
2. Verifying the fulfillment readiness of the fulfilling entity.
3. Establishing metering and billing.
4. Making self-service available.

A generic provider role can expand into service operator and service supporter also, as described in an earlier section.

7.1.2 Demand to Deployment: Creator Push

A service creator, without a business request, can choose to build and publish a service in the catalog. Usually these services are initiated as pioneers in providing the services to business. Push services are those that give an opportunity to attract the businesses that are looking for similar services as the ones just created. Push service attracts businesses to utilize and benefit from the services, and it will usually look to the future of service utilization.

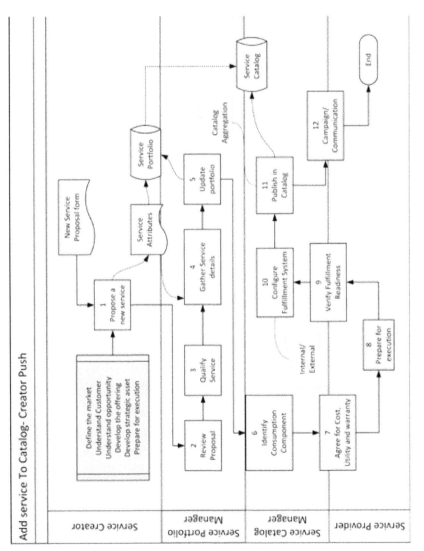

Figure 10: Catalog addition through creator push

When a service creator takes the risk of creating and publishing a service, there is no role for the business user in this creator-push process. The creator will take initiative to build after he or she has done the following:

1. Define the market: The creator will decide in which niche market he or she wants to play. This will be his or her core competency.
2. Understand the customer: Within the same market, the creator will analyze the customer's needs, biases, and brand affinity.
3. Understand the opportunity: After first two steps, the creator will have a very good understanding of the business opportunity for the market and the customer.
4. Develop offering: There could be one or more offering for the same service. It also has to do with the pricing strategy.
5. Develop strategic assets: The creator will invest the capability to building and keeping the service's usability. Most often, it will be a matter of people resources as the capital expenditures are usually eliminated because of the cloud.

At this point in time, the creator will be ready to take the proposal to the portfolio manager, who will qualify the service and update the service portfolio. When the service is ready and built, the catalog manager will identity consumption components and offering and publish it in the catalog. At this time, a fulfillment system will also be configured, and the architecture compliance checklist will be enforced.

7.1.3 Request to Fulfillment (R2F)

Once services are built and published in the catalog, the operational process Request-to-Fulfillment (R2F) will kick in. Figure 11 represents the process overview, and we envision a significantly different approach as compared to traditional ITSM.

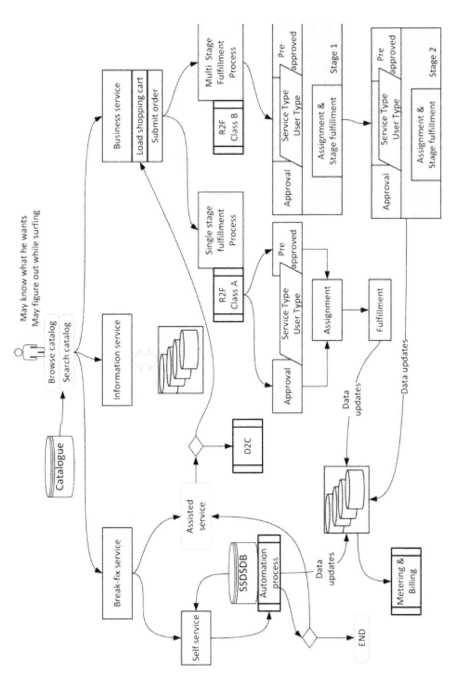

Figure 11: Request to fulfill flow

The industry trend suggests that almost everything will be self-service. Person-assisted service will be an exception. That means even a break-fix service will be an offering or self-service. Enterprise users need to reconcile with this scenario because they are accustomed to calling the Helpdesk and expecting a live agent to respond promptly. We believe that new-generation enterprise users are already reconciled to this scenario because they are experiencing this in the business world and welcoming it. Airlines, for example, have almost eliminated agent-assisted check-in.

When a user enters into the portal, he or she may know what he or she wants; otherwise, this person will figure it out while surfing. A good catalog navigation and presentation can simulate unsolicited demands. So browsing and searching catalogs is very critical for starting with a good user experience. Navigation will provide three different functional paths (break-fix service, information service, and business service), yet they will be seamless and appear as one. Users should be able to navigate across any path. The Amazon catalog is a very good example of this. If the user is choosing the break-fix service, the default option will always be self-service. Self-service will be delivered by SSDSDB and underline the automation processes. Each self-service component will have one record in SSDSDB and the automation process execution method. As the self-service is executed, execution records will update the fulfillment database that will be used for metering and billing. There may be instances where self-service may not be available or conclusive. This will lead to demand for assisted-service.

In assisted-service demands also, we see two scenarios. The first scenario will lead to the resolution of an incident or problem through the Detect-to-Correct (D2C) process. In the second scenario, the agent can just order on behalf of the user and trigger the R2F process.

The second path is a navigation of information service. This includes navigation of knowledge basis, variety of articles, and research and education on products and services. Cars.com is a good example of giving information on every manufacturer's car models. Although every manufacturer has its own catalog of cars, and the same information is replicated on cars.com, the comparison feature of cars.com is not given in any individual manufacturer's catalog. In the area of information technology, each cloud service provider maintains Cloud service catalog but a cloud service aggregator can aggregate all catalogs and can provide the comparison of each cloud service.

The third navigation path is browsing the business catalog, loading the shopping cart, and submitting the order. This will trigger a fulfillment process. We envision two kinds of fulfillment processes—single-stage fulfillment and multistage fulfillment. Single-stage fulfillment will be applicable for a fix price service that will go through the approval, assignment, and fulfillment steps. All services may not be fixed-price services. Variable price services will go through a multistage fulfillment process, where the first stage could be building the cost and estimates. The second step will be fulfillment on approval. It is important to note that the fulfiller in each stage could be different. For example, if a business is ordering an application enhancement service, it will usually provide the business requirement, which needs to be converted into a functional requirement and design before arriving at the cost. One team of business analysts could do this, and upon the approval of cost estimates, the enterprise will outsource the building to an external provider.

7.1.4 Detect to Correct

Detect-to-Correct (D2C) value stream, as defined in IT4IT reference architecture, is focused on keeping services running in production. D2C provides a framework for integrating monitoring, management, remediation, and other operational aspects. A conceptual understanding of D2C is given in the figure 12 for the people who want to relate it with traditional IT operations.

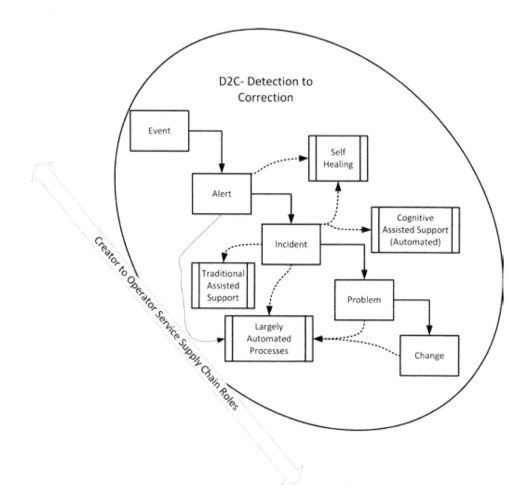

Figure 12: Detect to Correct (D2C)

The D2C Value Stream provides a framework for service operations integrating service monitoring, event, incident, problem, change control, configuration management, service remediation, and service-level functions. It incorporates a wide variety of sourcing methodologies across services, technologies, and processes. This value stream accommodates the technical interrelationships and interdependencies required to fix operational issues and improve the ability of the service operator to support business objectives.

7.1.5 Portfolio and Catalog Synchronization

Portfolios and catalogs are linked. In the traditional service management system, the portfolio includes all the chartered services in the pipeline, including the services not yet built, the services currently being built, the services that are deployed, and the services which have been retired. The catalog is the view of the portfolio, where the status of services is deployed.

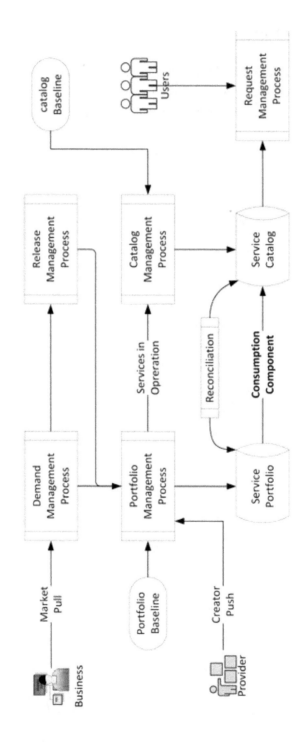

Figure 12: Portfolio and catalog synchronization

In the XaaS system, we continue with the same concept, but we also differentiate the content or the service properties that are stored in the catalog. We suggest that the catalog should include the service consumption component and/or specific offerings corresponding to a service in operation in the portfolio. A service in the portfolio may have multiple consumption components or offerings. This is important because the service consumer world revolves around the consumable components only. For example, the IaaS service in the portfolio will be represented by the virtual machine as the consumption component (requestable component or the item delivered for that service) in the catalog. There could be multiple templates or virtual machine configurations for an IaaS service in the portfolio. This is very similar to the request catalog. However, traditionally, request catalogs and portfolios are built independently, and there could be many services that can be requested through the catalog but not linked to the portfolio. This will pose a problem in the XaaS environment because you will not be able to segregate the roles in the service chain entity. Besides this, the service economics will be difficult to determine. We suggest including catalog and portfolio synchronization and a regular activity in lifecycle management processes.

7.1.6 User Registration and Profile Data Maintenance

If the service consumers are enterprise users (employees and contractors within an enterprise), then typical user profile management of traditional ITSM systems will apply. We have come across general deficiencies or weaknesses in the user profile management approach in a typical ITSM system, and we take this opportunity to provide basic guidance for this purpose. User profile is critical for effective service delivery as it controls the entitlement and cost accounting and a few other policies in the service delivery processes. An individual user in an enterprise is not required to register in the service management system, since the profile is created during the process of employee onboarding.

Every user in an enterprise will usually have two unique IDs: the employee ID that is created and maintained by the HR system and used for HR purposes such as payroll and the network ID that is maintained by the directory system and used for IT systems. It is extremely important to keep these two in synchronization, and a strong process should be built for this purpose. If an enterprise has an Identity Management (IdM) system, then such synchronization would become an integral part of the processes built around IdM data maintenance.

We classify user profile data into three categories. The first category includes the data elements that are fully in the control of the user, such as personal mobile phone number, address, and the like. Accuracy and currency of these data elements should be the responsibility of the individual user, and the user should be given tools at the portal to update the data directly.

The second category contains attributes that are controlled by the roles/group membership of the employee or by management based on the employee's role in the organization. Any update of these attributes of a user profile should be originated by the user and updated after validation by the appropriate authority. For example, the user role change can be verified by the manager and then updated in the profile.

The third category of the attributes is strictly controlled by HR systems, such as the cost center, hierarchy level, department code, and so on. Strong processes should be designed and maintained to keep the data in the ITSM system in sync with the HR system.

If the service user is a public user, then a registration process would create a user profile. The data elements will significantly change. The typical HR system data will be irrelevant and would be replaced by the data elements that we discussed in section 5. However, the principles of data element classification would still remain the same. Large data elements in user profiles will move under user control, such as credit card details for billing and payment.

7.1.7 Supplier Registration and Supplier Profile Data Maintenance

Supplier registration and supplier profile data maintenance are the important aspects of the service lifecycle management.

Earlier, we discussed consumer profiling and its purpose. Supplier profiling is similar to that. The term "supplier" is used for the multiple entities in the service chain that form the link to connect a service to the consumer. The purpose of supplier profiling is to do the SWOT analysis of a supplier to derive the best service from them and build and maintain a high-value catalog. This is usually done by the vendor management in any organization for an individual supplier to ensure that each supplier is in good standing. The big difference in supplier profiling in XaaS is that it is done in the context of the specific service and role of the supplier in that service chain. In this scheme, you may discover that, individually, two suppliers may be weak, but collectively they make a formidable combination that can add some strength to your catalog value chain.

8 XaaS Adoption

X aaS requires a paradigm shift in the mindset and thinking as well. The fact that the service catalog is the center of universe triggers the whole new considerations and approach.

1. The catalog manager and the portfolio manager role become critical and form an essential part of the organization structure. Hitherto, in traditional enterprise IT organizations, these roles were deemed as optional, and suddenly these roles come at the center stage. It is important to understand the responsibilities associated with these roles. A portfolio manager in the enterprise is a strategic role while catalog manager is operational role. Portfolio manager decides what kind of services will support the business strategy today and tomorrow and manages the service pipelines that is deployed and planned to be deployed. Catalog manager would decide what exactly the consumers are entitled to consume from a deployed service. Portfolio manager ensures that service is designed with the economic considerations of cost management and therefore price points and pricing model, while catalog manager ensures that measurement and billing for the service is in place and running as per chargeback model.

2. For every service, there ought to be a supply chain. Traditional provider/customer role are inadequate. Of course, an entity, internal or external, can assume multiple roles in the supply chain.

3. Every group in the IT org structure must have a mindset of a role in the service supply chain. It is no more a technology management job. You ought to know what service you are producing and who is your customer. For example, server administration/management is not a valid role. You would rather say I am providing IaaS service and application development team is my customer.

4. A customer cannot ask what he want but can order only the services that are standard and published in the catalog. For example, if server group is providing IaaS, you can choose the published configurations only (CPU, memory resources) but cannot define the requirement of your configurations.

Why do you need to adopt the XaaS model? Eventually, it will be difficult to do business if you do not. It is similar to the cloud adoption and migration. While cloud services such as IaaS, PaaS, and SaaS are already specific instances of XaaS, you need to plan for migration of all the services to the XaaS model—that is the wholesale catalog transformation in every stage of the service lifecycle from publishing to fulfillment. For this purpose, the services not defined and designed for an XaaS offering need to be reconstructed in the same way as applications that are not natively designed need reengineering to move onto the cloud.

1. Assessment/business case

Assessment of existing portfolios and catalogs in the context of the business strategy would answer the very first question: what does it mean to go to the XaaS model? There could be multiple drivers, such as:

1. Opportunity for chargeback and/or billing—An organization has decided to implement a chargeback and/or billing system for the business. Although the XaaS model is not necessary for chargeback, it would provide a lot of flexibility and wide options for chargeback. Billing will definitely require the aspects of metering at the individual consumer's end.

2. Opportunity for catalog building—Even for traditional services, the need for a professional catalog is becoming a necessity. Adoption of the XaaS model will automatically achieve this purpose.

3. Intent to outsource—Flexibility is significantly higher for outsourcing in the XaaS model as it discretely defines the roles in the service chain entity, and each role can be outsourced independently.

There may be other drivers also, such as manageability of services, establishing XaaS strategy for digital transformation, or just taking the advantage of the inherent benefits of XaaS.

2. Strategy and planning

Migration must be done in a strategic and methodical manner. Business drivers will formulate the strategy. Typical considerations fall into three areas: service reconstruction, service management system, and service chain entity reorganization. We envision a bi-modal service model in every organization. While the traditional services will continue as-is in its form and model, because there might be little justification or pressure to move to the XaaS model, the new services instrumental to digital transformation would be natively built and published in the XaaS model.

3. Service reconstruction

Table 3 will help identify kind of service reconstruction will be required. In some cases, it may be a matter of commercial reconstruction that is just presenting into usage-based contract, providing that other constructs such as metering are supporting that.

Service Attribute	Traditional Service Model	XaaS Service Model
Outcome	Undefined or vaguely defined	Crisply defined
Consumption method	Through controlled end points Some trends of BYOD	BYOD BYOA
Self-service	Nonexistent or limited	Largely self-service
Metering	Mostly nonexistent	Always, well-defined
Offering	Possibility of customization	Standard
SLA	Defined by customer	Defined by provider
Service chain entity	Undefined and may not be discrete	Discretely defined
Multivendor flexibility	Limited	Inherent by design

Table 3: How XaaS and traditional service compare

Breaking down an offering is also one of the possibilities of reconstruction when some of the offerings are trimmed and removed because of non-viability of SLA.

4. Service management system reengineering

Reconstruction of service for XaaS is one thing, but managing the lifecycle of the service in operation is another. In sections 5 and 6, we described typical service management systems and service management processes for XaaS. Traditional service management systems will require reengineering to manage the service lifecycle in XaaS mode. New requirements such as billing and self-service will create new processes and data-capturing mechanisms. The degree of reengineering would depend upon the existing state that will be determined in the assessment phase. Reengineering requirements will also be driven by the reconstruction of service; for example, each of the self-service, SLA measurements, and role segregation in the service chain entity could be a huge reengineering effort. Sometimes it may be easier to build a new-generation XaaS service management system than to enhance a legacy system.

5. Service chain entity formalization or reshuffling

Discrete definition of service chain entities is an essential element of service architecture for XaaS. When service is reconstructed, discrete entities will be defined and newer roles will emerge. Even though the number of entities remains the same as they were in traditional service, role mapping will still be required, and one entity can take multiple roles. The gray area between the roles will vanish (another benefit), and a cohesive end-to-end service chain will emerge.

6. Continual transition of services

Not every service could be in XaaS mode. Organizations can maintain bimodal Service Catalogs; however, new services should be natively designed for the XaaS model. Many items appearing in traditional Service Catalogs are actually products (for example, standard laptops), but the XaaS system can act like a conveyor belt upon which the delivery of a product can also ride.

Productizing the Service Is Key for XaaS Adoption

In section 2.4, we mentioned the characteristics of productization. Even though the fundamental characteristic of a service is its intangibility, productization helps to bring a sense of tangibility to it. This will help to apply age-old, proven, and mature business practices that are in use for product businesses. Let us compare the product delivery chain with the service chain entity.

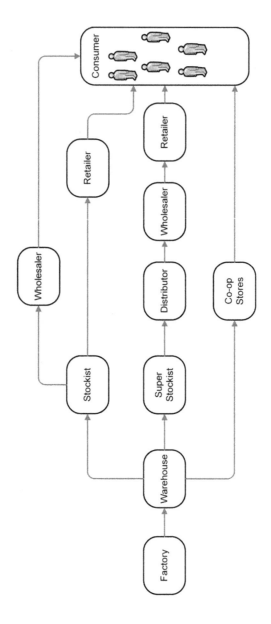

Figure 14: Old model of consumer good delivery chain—compare it with the XaaS service chain in figure 6

This is how Amazon has collapsed the delivery chain:

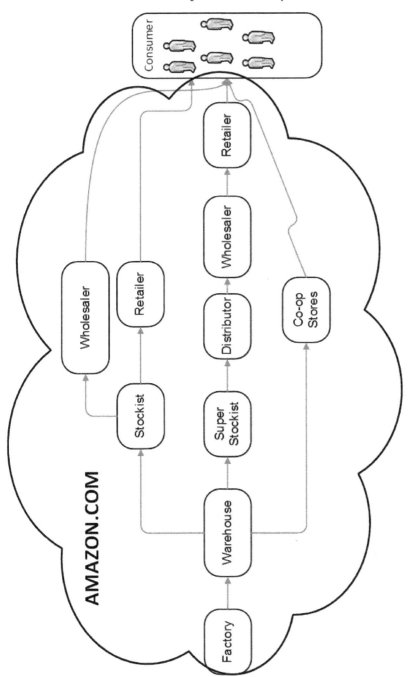

Figure 15: FCMG delivery chain collapse by Amazon

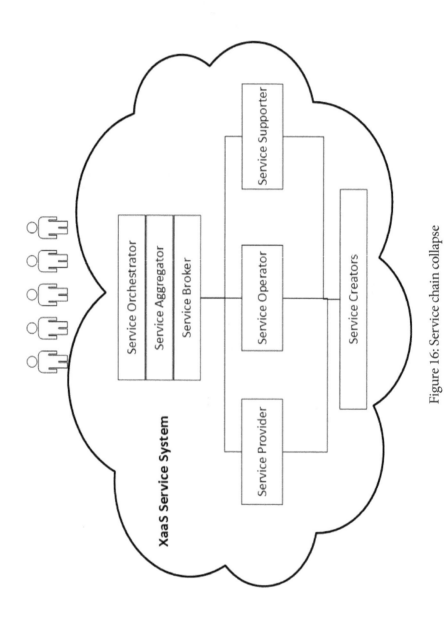

Figure 16: Service chain collapse

Value Addition Imperative for XaaS Adoption

Every entity in the chain must add value. Why would a consumer not directly buy from the creator if the middleman does not have any value addition? The value addition in the FCMG model pictured above is very well understood and recognized. The same principles will apply for the XaaS model also.

Cultural aspects and change management for XaaS Adoption

New generation of workforce (born digital of digital native) is increasing in the enterprise. This generation is already using technology much more effectively in day-to-day life. The population that is joining the workforce has grown up with the current state of ubiquitous computing and communications, and power user of technology like smartphones, social media and continuous online. This generation has less recognition of geographical, cultural and workplace boundaries and more inclined to collaborate with the help of technology. We also have "digital settlers" - people who didn't grow up with the current technologies but who have adopted them and adapted to the changing environment. Digital native and digital settlers are already accustomed to XaaS and self-service models and this is the default standard for them. This generation is forced to move backward in adopting the old technology of enterprise IT. Is it not better to force old generation to learn from new generation and force them to move forward in the new model? This will require investment in redesigning the traditional services but that is inevitable anyway.

But we do have "digital immigrants" - who grew up without the current technologies and who have come to them so late that they are still largely baffled by them. We still see the old mind set of traditional user support in enterprises and noticing a strong resistance in the "old" generation that is accustomed of using client server technology to adopt to BYOD, mobility and service support model as against user support. The old generation still seeks handholding from service desk for their IT needs. In order to serve the born digital population in the enterprise, born digital material and born digital service development/transformation is imperative.the born digital population in the enterprise, born digital material and born digital service development/transformation is imperative.

9 ITIL, IT4IT, COBIT, and XaaS

A strong need for service management frameworks and models emerged in the 1990s with the evolution of service management as an important discipline. Industry-led and vendor-led models (for example, IBM and HP) started emerging. Two of the most popular frameworks/models (ITIL and COBIT) and one relatively new model (IT4IT) that is rapidly getting noticed are included in this discussion and reviewed where these require adjustments for use in the XaaS model.

ITIL

ITIL is the most widely accepted approach to ITSMin the world. It provides guidance to organizations and individuals on how to use IT as a tool to facilitate business change, transformation, and growth. ITIL defines the five-stage lifecycle of services and best practices around each stage; these are currently detailed within five core publications:

1. Service strategy
2. Service design
3. Service transition
4. Service operation
5. Continual service improvement

These five volumes map the entire ITIL service lifecycle, beginning with the identification of customer needs and drivers of IT requirements through to the design and implementation of the service, and, finally, the monitoring and improvement phase of the service.

COBIT

COBIT is the framework for the governance and management of enterprise IT. COBIT 5 is the current version of the framework that assists enterprises in achieving their objectives for the governance and management of enterprise IT. It is designed to help enterprises by maintaining a balance between realizing benefits and optimizing risk levels and resource use of information technology. COBIT 5 enables IT to be governed and managed in a holistic manner for the entire enterprise, taking in the full end-to-end business and IT functional areas of responsibility and considering the IT-related interests of internal and external stakeholders. COBIT 5 is generic and useful for enterprises of all sizes, all industry verticals, and all organization types.

IT4IT

The Open Group IT4IT standard comprises reference architecture and a value-chain-based operating model for managing the business of IT. It provides prescriptive guidance on how to design, procure, and implement the functionality needed to run IT. The end-to-end, how-to emphasis of the IT value chain and IT4IT also enables the state of services that IT delivers to be systematically tracked across the service lifecycle. IT4IT defines four value streams supported by reference architecture to drive efficiency and agility. The four value streams are:

1. Strategy to Portfolio
2. Request to Fulfill
3. Requirement to Deploy
4. Detect to Correct

Each IT value stream is centered on a key aspect of the service model, the essential data objects (information model), and functional components (functional model) that support it. Together, the four value streams play a vital role in helping IT control the service model as it advances through its lifecycle.

ITIL	COBIT	IT4IT
Process lead approach for Service management Primarily a service management framework	Governance and risk-management approach for IT service management. Primarily an IT governance and control framework	Value-chain-based approach for service management Primarily an IT value-chain model and reference architecture
Five lifecycle states 1. Strategy 2. Design 3. Transition 4. Operation 5. Improvement Total of twenty-seven processes across all lifecycle states	Five domains 1. APO (align, plan, and organize) 2. BAI (build, acquire, and implement) 3. DSS (deliver, service, and support) 4. MEA (monitor, evaluate, and assess) 5. EDM (evaluate, direct, and monitor) Total of thirty-seven processes (thirty-two management and five governance-domain EDM) across all domains	Four value-chain streams 1. S2P (strategy to portfolio) 2. R2D (requirement to deploy) 3. R2F (request to fulfill) 4. D2C (detect to correct) Value streams mapped to four phases (plan, build, deliver, and run) on the foundation of support activities in five functional areas. Processes implied in each value stream component

ITIL	COBIT	IT4IT
Best practices and guidelines, nonprescriptive, focus on management and delivery of IT services	Focus on IT control objectives, captures the essence of other IT frameworks, nonprescriptive	Process agnostic architecture, data-driven, focuses on business—IT alignment, prescriptive model
Provides guidance on how ITSM processes should be managed and executed	Describes what control objectives are required for processes and why they are requireda	Positions IT as a business function and provides data and artifacts required to manage services

Table 4: Comparison of industry service management frameworks

ITIL for XaaS Model

ITIL V2 was published in 2002. During those times, even virtualization was virtually nonexistent in the enterprise environment, and concept of cloud was not even born. Two-tier and three-tier client service architecture was the de facto standard throughout the enterprise IT environment, and ITIL V2 was very good at addressing that. Later, ITIL V3 was released in 2009, but the core service management operational components remained unchanged; these were incident management, problem management, event management, change management, CSIP, and so on. So ITIL has some natural deficiency by design for the XaaS environment.

Although ITIL has defined the service portfolio and Service atalog, it does not define the properties of service related to consumption components and consumption models. Besides this, it does not have the concept of expanded service chain entity; it has a fixed-value chain—that is, stakeholders in the definitions of SLA, OLA, and UC. The concept of cost models and chargeback does exist in ITIL, but metering and billing like the utility model are not explicit. Self-service is the cornerstone of XaaS, and ITIL is not very clear about it. Many organizations that have done the ITIL implementation claim the implementation of self-service, but that is a limited implementation. Most of them are limited to ordering from portal and knowledge search. XaaS is not only self-service for order but also self-service for fulfillment and resolution of issues as well.

Other service properties are very well covered in ITIL such as CI, service function, SLA, and more. These can be used in the XaaS model also. Heavy considerations for user environments and service desks in ITIL are diluted because of the BYOD and self-service imperatives of XaaS. In summary, ITIL requires enhancements (and probably radical changes) to apply it to the XaaS model.

COBIT for XaaS

ISACA has published a guide, "Control and Assurance in Cloud," that claims that COBIT 5 can be extended for use toward cloud governance mainly because it:
• is platform-agnostic, both in type and complexity;
• has sufficient depth to address nearly all the technical aspects of cloud computing;
• provides clearly defined process activity measures.

Several points discussed in the ITIL section above apply to COBIT also. In our opinion, COBIT is extremely risk-management-focused and very tedious to implement. Besides this, it is natively designed with the consideration of technology management and governance in the old era, when agility, devops, and microservice concepts—which are the cornerstone of the XaaS world—were nonexistent. The concept of service architecture is missing altogether. Besides this, the security and compliance focus of COBIT is radically different because security by design of the service is the new security approach. Security by design (SbD) is a security-assurance approach that formalizes service design, automates security controls, and streamlines auditing. Instead of relying on auditing security retroactively, SbD provides security control built in throughout the XaaS service management process. Therefore, from a GRC perspective, COBIT will hold its ground in the XaaS world, but from a service management perspective, it would require significant (or radical) overhauls and enhancements.

IT4IT for XaaS

IT4IT is newer in the industry and was developed in the era when cloud computing was also emerging. Therefore, several concepts of IT4IT are natively suitable for the XaaS world. The IT4IT reference architecture includes the information model and integration model, which is based on a system of records fabric. There are more than thirty key data objects and functional components with prescribed data flow, attributes, and relationships.

The lifecycle starts with a conceptual service model, which includes why we need a service, who the customers are, how much it might cost, and what the benefits are. The logical service model is a view of the service in terms of the system design and capabilities that are needed to operate the service. The realized service model is where a service is released and available in a service catalog for subscription. In our opinion, it is ahead of other frameworks in its suitability of XaaS. We have used several criteria of IT4T in section 6 of this book.

10 Annexure

10.1 Orchestration and Choreography in IT Operations and Service Management

A compared to other industries, Information Technology is relatively newer industry and developed its technology dictionary with relatively large number of acronyms. When it uses well-understood generic language dictionary words in the context of IT, it sometimes creates its own interpretation or meaning that might puzzle the original subject readers. Orchestration and choreography are two such words which are very well defines and understood in context of their original subject- music and dance respectively, but very badly "re-defined" and interpreted in the context of IT. In fact there is widely inconsistent subjective interpretation of these words in IT operations.

In this paper we shall provide our interpretation of these two terminologies along with the related terminologies and then provide our opinion on their functional importance i.e. what function they represent and what purpose they achieve in modern day IT and business operations and service management. We shall attempt to maintain the integrity of the original dictionary meaning of these words in our definition.

Choreography is a matter of composing the sequence of steps and moves for a dance that can be performed *autonomously* by an individual dancer in the group. Choreographer does not control or direct during the run time performance of the dance. The onus of producing the desired effect is not on the choreographer but remains with the individual performer. Choreography, in the context of IT, is thus a plan and control of operations in *autonomous* manner where individual objects of control (task or process or service) interacts and synchronize with each other according to the sequences designed and learned in earlier stage of the operations. The onus of producing the desired outcome remains on individual element (task, process or service).

Orchestration is the matter of arranging and directing the music score to produce the desire effect and melody. Orchestrator assigns the different musical instruments and corresponding musical notes to individual musician and the onus of producing the desired effect is on orchestrator not on the individual performer. In the context of IT operation and service management, orchestration is to coordinate and direct the operation in *autocratic* manner and the onus of delivering the desired outcome is with the orchestrator.

Choreography and orchestration can be seen in tandem in all Bollywood songs that is a combination of music and dance and where the choreography is synchronized with the orchestration of music.

Following table summarizes the difference

Orchestration	Choreography
Autocratic	Autonomous
Onus of outcome on orchestrator	Onus of outcome on individual element
External and business facing	Internal and technology facing
User experience is the goal	Speed and agility is the goal
Effectiveness focus	Efficiency focus
Across domains	Within Domain
Directive SIAM	Control Tower SIAM

10.2 Importance and use cases of Orchestration

XaaS environment composite service

A service in the service catalog may be composed of multiple services and requires orchestration across multiple service providers for delivery/fulfillment. We see these examples in business all the time. Travel service for example offers airline, hotel and car rental booking. In IT operations, especially in XaaS model like PaaS and SaaS provisioning require orchestration across multiple elements.

In a typical scenario, enterprise would procure- for its employees- e-mail as a service (say Microsoft), personal storage service as a service (say Google Drive or Drop box), and provides a virtual desktop and retains the domain authentication and directory service in-house. The HR becomes a service integrator for "New Hire" service. The execution of this service requires sequential execution of individual service providers – Domain account is created, that triggers e-mail account provision and with that e-mail account as an ID, Google drive is provisioned and also the virtual desktop is provisioned. There could be manual service execution also if there is a physical laptop that needs to be delivered and added to the domain.

SIAM

A prominent example of orchestration is Service Integration and Management (SIAM) and research analysts like Gartner have repeatedly emphasized that the multivendor model for IT services is complex and requires orchestration between vendors that are often fierce competitors. This orchestration requires the enterprise to establish a multi-sourcing delivery model that provides visibility and transparency into multiple vendor systems and processes. A SIAM service provider orchestrates the operational activities across multiple service providers. (Method of activity does not matter- Activities can be manual or automated or both).

Typical example is a critical incident management process; where critical incident manager is an orchestrator and directs different service provide to act together to restore the services.

Might of orchestration in the business

Two examples are worth mentioning to illustrate the might of orchestration in the business- Uber and Amazon. Uber is the largest personal transportation company in the world but it does not own a single taxi nor does it employ a single driver. All it does is the orchestration between the various elements of the services. Similarly Amazon is the largest retailer without owning a single retail store. Amazon also achieved this feet by the virtue of orchestration between the consumer and supplier.

10.3 Importance and use cases of Choreography

Monitoring

Monitoring of a landscape, which consists of systems, networks, composite applications, containers running microservices etc. has a big potential of using choreography driven model. Today monitoring systems are controlled centrally via a management server, which becomes the bottleneck in a dynamic microservices environment. Having monitoring itself running as microservices, which choreograph themselves with other monitoring services across the landscape and communicate using RESTful APIs could make the overall delivery of the service more agile. When we combine this with an orchestrated service layer we get the benefit of scalability and control achieved.

MicroServices

Implementing microservices fundamentally means we bring in a significant layer of autonomy at the business technical service layer to allow services to choreograph themselves based on the service boundaries coded into the system and the top level composite service catalog is the only orchestrated entity which then let the respective microservices operate and manage their I/O in a self managed way. When we start to deploy microservices within containers as fully enclosed runtimes then the multiplier effect of choreography becomes exponential.

10.4 Related definitions

Process automation

A business process or an IT process can be executed without human intervention. This is very common in every IT operations and service management these days and there are in built features in all ITSM tools for notifications, approvals, assignment, provisioning etc.

Task Automation

Task automation is the execution of a discrete task in a process. For example purging a log file, deleting the history on log out etc.

Process orchestration vs task automation

Processes encompass a value chain, which has many touch points within the enterprise IT landscape. The concept of BPM (business process management) has been prevalent in the business integration layer. We see the application of the same concept but in a more agile and integration-oriented play within the service integration domain. Process orchestration enables integration of multiple process areas and function areas across the extended enterprise to allow seamless flow of operational pipeline across multiple providers. Process orchestration focuses in "what". It is focused on results or outcome of the value chain. With the advent of complex architectures like Cloud OS, Software Defined Data Centers, etc., we feel that having a domain specific orchestrator and an enterprise Process Orchestrator connected to a core ITSM system will be essential for service integration. Task automation is focused on sequencing of activities/procedures required to achieve the output, which is the how. Multiple outputs might be part of a larger outcome. Successful task automation doesn't imply successful process orchestration. Task automation visibility to the enterprise process orchestration is the key outcome of this integration.

Acronyms used

BT	Business Technology
CI	Configuration Item
CIM	Common Information Model
CMDB	Configuration Management Database
COBIT	Control Objective for Information Technology
EDP	Electronic Data Processing
IOT	Internet of Things
IT	Information Technology
ITIL	Information Technology Infrastructure Library
ITSM	Information Technology Service Management
MIS	Management Information System
MVP	Minimum Viable Product
OT	Operation Technology
ROCE	Return on Capital Employed
ROI	Return on Investment
SIAM	Service Integration and Management
SSDSDB	Self Service Delivery and Support Database
TCP/IP	Transport Control Protocol/Internet Protocol
XaaS	Anything as a Service

About the authors

Prafull Verma

Prafull Verma has a bachelor's degree in electronics and communication engineering and has over thirty years' experience in the area of electronic data processing and information technology. He started his career in India in the area of electronic data processing systems and later moved to the United States in 1997. During the past thirty years, he has worked on diversified areas in computer science and information technologies. Some of his key experience areas are the design and implementation of heterogeneous networks, midrange technical support management, end-user service management and design, and the implementation and management of process-driven ITSM systems.

Prafull has acquired a unique blend of expertise in integrated areas of tools, process, governance, operations, and technology. He is the author of several methodology and frameworks for IT service management that include multi- vendor ITIL frameworks, ITSM for cloud computing and Service Integration.

Prafull's competencies and specializations include the area of merging engineering with service management, as this book manifests, and outsourcing business management.

Currently, Prafull is working for HCL Technologies Ltd as Fellow and Chief Architect. He is the global leader for DRYICE Service Orchestration Business Unit in HCL. He is also serving member of the product advisory council of ServiceNow, the industry leading ITSM platform.

Kalyan Kumar

Kalyan Kumar B. (KK) is the Global CTO of HCL Technologies. KK leads 'Global Product and Technology Organization' and is the leader of DRYiCE Business Unit, a unified autonomics and orchestration platform business, which is the core foundation of the 21st Century Enterprise. Additionally, he oversees the cloud services business unit across all service lines within HCL.

KK is responsible for creating key frameworks such as 'DRYiCE Autonomics & Orchestration Framework'. Also, he has conceptualized HCL's XaaS-based DRYiCE platform that incorporates holistic automation capabilities across Integrated Technology & Operations Automation, Cloud & DevOps Automation, Robotic Process Automation, which leverages Artificial Intelligence & Robotics across all disciplines, including Machine Learning, Neuro-Linguistic Processing (NLP), Cognitive Conversations, Neural Networks, Computer Vision, Cognitive Process Automation, Unified Orchestration and Choreography integrated via XaaS Service Exchange. Under his leadership, DRYiCE NLP has been awarded with the prestigious AIconics Best Innovation in the NLP Category at the AI Summit held in London.

In his free time Kalyan likes to jam with his band Contraband as a drummer / percussionist and reviews Consumer Technology Gadgets and follows Cricket Games and also coaches Young Adults on Cricket . Kalyan lives in London, United Kingdom with his family.

KK can be followed on Twitter @KKLIVE and at Linkedin (http://www.linkedin. com/in/kalyankumar).

From the same Authors

Process Excellence for IT Operations: a Practical Guide for IT Service Process Management

Authored by Mr Prafull Verma, Authored by Mr Kalyan Kumar B

List Price: $29.95
6" x 9" (15.24 x 22.86 cm)
Black & White on White paper
332 pages
Process Excellence for IT
Operations
ISBN-13: 978-0615877525
(Custom Universal)
ISBN-10: 0615877524
BISAC: Computers /
Information Technology

As the title suggests, the book is providing a practical guidance on managing the processes for IT Services. There are lot of guidance available on technology management in IT industry but this book is focusing on technology independent service management. The book will be addressed to all IT people from a process practitioner perspective, however, the fundamentals are presented in simplistic terms, and therefore it should be useful to all IT people. It will describe the process engineering concept and how it can be applied to IT Service Management. This is not about the industry standard framework such as ITIL and COBIT but about the common processes that are generally used in real life operations. This book does not focus on any technology.

Foundation of IT Operations Management: Event Monitoring and Controls

Authored by Mr Prafull Verma, Authored by Mr Kalyan Kumar B

List Price: $15.95
6" x 9" (15.24 x 22.86 cm)
Black & White on White paper
138 pages
Foundation Of IT Operation
ISBN-13: 978-0692205709
(Custom Universal)
ISBN-10: 0692205705
BISAC: Computers /
Information Technology

In IT operations, event monitoring and control - where you continuously monitor the health of IT infrastructure and take proactive measures to prevent the interruptions in IT services- is dominated by tools and technology but there is a meticulous process behind it. This book tries to demystify the underlying process for this kind of operation management. There are lot many books on service management but those books do not cover this subject adequately and leave this area to be addressed by tools and technology. Tools vendor on the other hand, focus on the tool part, leaving the process aspect to the service management professionals. This book fills in the void and connects both, the process and the tools to provide a holistic view. The book takes an educative tone and written primarily for IT generalist and not for the tool experts, although it would give a new perspective to tool experts also.

Service Integration: A Practical Guide to Multivendor Service Management

Authored by Mr Prafull Verma, Authored by Mr Kalyan Kumar B

List Price: $15.95
6" x 9" (15.24 x 22.86 cm)
Black & White on White paper
138 pages
Foundation Of IT Operation
ISBN-13: 978-0692205709
(Custom Universal)
ISBN-10: 0692205705
BISAC: Computers /
Information Technology

SERVICE INTEGRATION
A PRACTICAL GUIDE TO MULTIVENDOR
SERVICE MANAGEMENT
Prafull Verma and Kalyan Kumar

This book is intended to present simplified guide for IT generalists who are new to the service integration subject. The purpose of this book is to educate all IT professionals with the basic concepts of the service integration. Additionally the purpose is to provide the core guidance and foundation guidance to Service Management professionals, upon which they can build and implement the service integration in their environment.

Software Asset Management: Understanding and implementing an optimal solution

Authored by Mr Prafull Verma, Authored by Mr Kalyan Kumar B

List Price: $15.95
6" x 9" (15.24 x 22.86 cm)
Black & White on White paper
148 pages
Software Asset Management
ISBN-13: 978-0692324264
(Custom Universal)
ISBN-10: 0692324267
BISAC: Computers /
Information Technology

Software asset management (SAM) is an essential need for all IT organizations, not just because of the cost of software but also because of the potential litigation of copyright violation for use of unlicensed software. Most of the organizations deploy tools for software asset management, but fail to achieve the desired goals because tools are a small part of the holistic solution. This books explains the underlying complexity of SAM and includes all aspects of SAM solution that includes solution architecture, the SAM processes, tools and function and provide a guideline to develop, build and operate an optimal solution

Foundation of Intelligent IT Operations: CMDB and Service Maps

Authored by Mr. Prafull Verma, Authored by Mr. Mohan Kewalramani, Authored by Mr. Kalyan Kumar

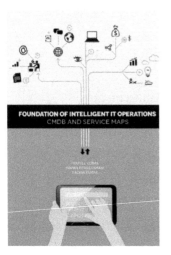

List Price: $15.95
6" x 9" (15.24 x 22.86 cm)
Black & White on White paper
172 pages
Software Asset Management
ISBN-13: 978-0692380925
(Custom Universal)
ISBN-10: 0692380922
BISAC: Computers /
Information Technology

The scale of enterprise IT environments are growing rapidly and computing resources are deployed in abundance. Consequently, management of IT operations gets increasingly complex. Service Maps and the CMDB (Configuration Management Database) are key tools to enable an organization to intelligently manage the complexity of dependencies and relationships between components. Theoretically, this sounds reasonable and easily achievable, especially since the concept of a CMDB was introduced in ITIL v2 more than a decade ago and the assumption is that almost all organizations that have adopted ITIL would have a CMDB and be delivering on its intended objectives. The reality is far removed from theory though.

Designing, implementing and maintaining a sensible CMDB that is fit for purpose and does not end up being a project set up for failure requires more than just theoretical knowledge. Additionally, with the rapid adoption of cloud computing, Internet of Things (IoT) and other

135

disruptive technologies in an increasingly complex multi supplier environment with implementations of "Service Integration and Management (SIAM)", the old school vision of the CMDB needs to be designed with a renewed perspective to keep it relevant to our IT environments today.

This book tries to educate IT generalists with the basics of a CMDB and service maps without the need for understanding technology or any specialist tools, while trying to guide IT service management professionals to build an intelligent information system that produces real benefits to support the management of IT services by having a reliable and enriched source of information, that helps in making better, more informed decisions.

www.ingramcontent.com/pod-product-compliance
Lightning Source LLC
Chambersburg PA
CBHW071205050326

40689CB00011B/2248